Why
Do You
Trouble This
Woman?

Why Do You Trouble This Woman?

Women and the Spiritual Exercises of St. Ignatius of Loyola

ANNE ARABOME, SSS

Paulist Press
New York / Mahwah, NJ

Library of Congress Cataloging-in-Publication Data
Names: Arabome, Anne, author.
Title: Why do you trouble this woman? : women and the spiritual exercises of St. Ignatius of Loyola / Anne Arabome, SSS.
Description: New York / Mahwah, NJ : Paulist Press, [2022] | Summary: "An insightful, engaging, and theologically based narrative examination of Ignatian spirituality and its transformative gifts for contemporary women who are inspired to engage in a life-changing personal pilgrimage with the Spiritual Exercises of St. Ignatius of Loyola"— Provided by publisher.
Identifiers: LCCN 2022019087 (print) | LCCN 2022019088 (ebook) | ISBN 9780809156160 (paperback) | ISBN 9780809187782 (ebook)
Subjects: LCSH: Catholic women—Religious life. | Ignatius, of Loyola, Saint, 1491–1556. Exercitia spiritualia. | Spiritual exercises.
Classification: LCC BX2353 .A73 2022 (print) | LCC BX2353 (ebook) | DDC 248.8/43—dc23/eng/20220801
LC record available at https://lccn.loc.gov/2022019087
LC ebook record available at https://lccn.loc.gov/2022019088

ISBN 978-0-8091-5616-0 (paperback)
ISBN 978-0-8091-8778-2 (e-book)

Published by Paulist Press
997 Macarthur Boulevard
Mahwah, New Jersey 07430
www.paulistpress.com

Printed and bound in the
United States of America

*To Mrs. Gloria Arabome and Mrs. Roseline Orobator
Two African mothers and theologians who remind me of
the Mothers of Ignatius of Loyola and Mothers of the
Spiritual Exercises by their example of embodied,
imaginative, and contemplative spirituality*

Contents

Foreword by Lisa Sowle Cahill ix

Acknowledgments xiii

Introduction: Woman Trouble xvii

1. In the Beginning Were Women 1

2. Finding God in All Things...22

3. Women's Bodies and the God of Our Bodies........................43

4. The Gift and the God of Imagination 67

5. The God-Place of Storytelling 89

6. Contemplative Awakening, Awareness, and Action.......... 110

Conclusion: An Unfolding Story.. 131

Notes.. 139

Foreword
Lisa Sowle Cahill

Although I am fortunate to count her as a personal friend, I first became acquainted with Anne Arabome through her writings. About a decade ago, while searching for course materials on African women and the Catholic Church, I serendipitously uncovered an essay developing a Nigerian perspective on "uses and abuses" of role expectations for women. The wonderful thing about this essay—as about all Anne's writings—is that she pulls no punches in diagnosing exactly where Catholicism and culture fall short, yet maintains a no less generous, hopeful spirit regarding the hidden blessings and future joys a living faith conveys to women. As she relates at the beginning of the above essay, the symbol of her religious order, the Sisters of Social Service, is the Holy Spirit imaged as a dove. By the power of the Holy Spirit, Anne trusts absolutely that both men and women are being and will be liberated by the equal discipleship and ministry of women in the Roman Catholic Church. The present book exudes this same confidence and gladness of heart, along with compassion for women who have yet to recognize God's delight in and call for them, and for the men—including Ignatius!—whose vision is shaded by the sexist blinders that longstanding traditions impose. According to Anne, the "enchanting and mystical" depths of the *Spiritual Exercises* can be life-transforming for all.

Ignatius empowers women (and men) to see God and God's purposes in all things, to listen with openness and imagination to the voice of God in their own experiences, to understand that their own deepest being and desires are created and called by God. Ignatius's "Principle and Foundation" is to desire and choose only what leads us to God. Anne makes a link to women's storytelling—how does my "story" reveal God's purposes for me? Discernment of the choices and actions to which contemplation leads depends on self-knowledge.

Ignatius's spirituality puts the body and embodiment in a central place. The body is our way of connecting to our environment—through senses and feelings, being in a concrete place and specific relations, knowing and loving holistically as the persons we are created concretely to be. This is a freeing and uplifting message for women whose cultures communicate that women's bodies make women lesser than men, subject to male control; or who struggle with cultural body images that convey just as clearly that their embodied being is inadequate. Ignatian spirituality places the experience of God in the midst of life as it is. "For the woman of the *Exercises*," promises Anne Arabome, "it can be life changing to begin to see her life take shape as an oasis of infinite love!"

Yet, despite the level of respect and appreciation St. Ignatius rightly commands from admirers and followers, it won't do to downplay the *Exercises*' "male-dominated" biases, stereotypes, and angles of vision. Ignatius even compares the evil spirit to a woman, and warns readers away from the weakness, credulity, and fickleness of women. His line of vision is persistently androcentric. One of the first pieces of advice he gives readers of the *Exercises* is to cultivate a healthy sense of shame, originally directed perhaps to assertive men tempted by arrogance and presumption. How appropriate is this counsel, protests

Foreword

Anne, for women who have internalized distorted images of women's sexuality, bodies, and desires? Could the cultivation of shame reinforce the cultural prescriptions and proscriptions that undermine women's trust in their connection to God, their confident ability to hear and answer the divine presence in their lives?

Surprisingly and creatively, Anne finds liberating potential even in Ignatius's advice on shame. Virtuous shame as he defines it is *healthy* shame—grounded in a true and accurate perception of one's own capacities, limits, failures, and potential achievements as a child of God. The precondition of healthy shame is healthy self-respect. A prior knowledge of one's God-given dignity allows one to recognize when one has lived up to one's calling and when one has not—whether shame is appropriate or should be resisted. Healthy shame presupposes the ability to recognize when the demands of another drown out the gift of God's calling and to confront unjust relationships. This is essential to the process of spiritual discovery that is at the heart of the *Exercises*.

One of the most engaging parts of *Why Do You Trouble This Woman?* is Anne Arabome's imaginative reconstruction of Ignatius's relationship to the many women in his life and her voicing of their views of and advice for him. Those to some degree familiar with this saint's biography may realize that his mother died when he was an infant; that he was nurtured in his early years by his nurse, the blacksmith's wife, Maria de Garin; and that he was cared for after his combat injury by his sister-in-law Magdalena. Less familiar perhaps are Inez Pasqual, who helped Ignatius as a young pilgrim discover his mission; and the women (especially Princess Juana of Spain and Isabel Roser, an early benefactress) who were briefly associates or members of the Society of Jesus. These and other women left their mark on Ignatius and on the *Exercises*. Anne imagines that Ignatius would attest, "Their feminine way of perceiving the Spirit alive and active in the world was a gift to me."

The dialogue and mutual influence of Ignatius and women continues in the life of the *Exercises*, every time they are read and appropriated by women, occasion the companionship of women and men who follow the *Exercises* together, or provoke new reflections on the presence of God in the hearts and lives of women today, in contexts and cultures far from Ignatius's original setting. Anne Arabome is an exceptional weaver and proclaimer of this ongoing Ignatian tradition. Her spiritual liveliness, common sense, generosity of spirit, healing compassion, and joyful exuberance make this introduction to the *Spiritual Exercises of St. Ignatius of Loyola* an indispensable guide for all who would turn to Ignatius's spiritual classic for consolation, encouragement, guidance, and renewal.

Acknowledgments

I am profoundly grateful to the editorial director, Paul McMahon, and the editorial team at Paulist Press for accepting this work for publication. From the onset of this collaborative venture, Paul and his team radiated deep kindness, professionalism, and respect that encouraged me to entrust my story to them.

My gratitude also goes to Sr. Mary Murphy, FCJ, who introduced me to women's spirituality in the *Spiritual Exercises* at St. Beuno's Jesuit Spirituality Centre in St. Asaph, North Wales, and to Prof. Tina Beattie, who inspired me to include and affirm the voices of women in theology, church, and religion during the course of my studies at the University of Roehampton, London.

I am grateful to Spiritual Directors International (SDI) for the invitation to share my reflections on Ignatian spirituality with their global members and network. It was a great platform and a unique opportunity to present and test my ideas.

My dear friends, Mary Ann Archer and Kathy Lilla Cox, have never relented in their support and encouragement for my writing. These gifted theologians and spiritual companions shared my quest to breathe new life into the *Spiritual Exercises* and to make it a home for women.

Why Do You Trouble This Woman?

I owe a great deal of gratitude to my colleagues at Marquette University, Milwaukee, Wisconsin. The Faber Center for Ignatian Spirituality is an oasis of serenity and a font of creativity for the dynamics of Ignatian spirituality, thanks to the courageous and visionary leadership of Dr. Michael Dante and the support of Sue Cirillo. Your kindness and openness to me make it easy to do ministry at Marquette.

My sincere thanks to Rev. Jim Voiss, the Vice President for Mission and Ministry, and all his team, who collaborate with the Faber Center to create spiritual ministries that support the mission of Marquette.

I am deeply grateful to all the Marquette Spiritual Sisters, who gather weekly to reflect on and to share the gifts and beauty of women in the *Spiritual Exercises* and in the Ignatian tradition. It is a consolation to journey with you.

Thank you to all the administrators, deans, faculty, and staff who have supported my ministry at Marquette. I desist from mentioning names; you are too many to mention. Know that I carry you all in my heart and prayers.

Special thanks to the Jesuits of Dr. E. J. O'Brien Jesuit Residence at Marquette. Your kind and gracious hospitality always makes feel at home.

My loving family, my mom, Mrs. Gloria Arabome, my late dad, Prince Joe Arabome, and all my siblings and their families, have been an incredible and amazing gift to me from God. My love for you knows no bounds.

I am grateful to my community of the Sisters of Social Service in Los Angeles, California, especially Sr. Michele Walsh, SSS, and Sr. Rochelle Mitchell, SSS, for believing in me and inviting me to serve the community with my talents and gifts. Among my sisters, it is to Sr. Deborah Lorentz, SSS, that I offer my deepest thanks for never failing to be there for me. Words are not enough to express my affection for and gratitude to you.

Acknowledgments

This litany of gratitude culminates in my joyous expression of appreciation and gratitude for Oghomwen n'Oghomwen Agbonkhianmeghe E. Orobator, SJ, my soulmate and dear friend, whose presence in my life reflects the face of God's love. Like the women who journeyed with Ignatius of Loyola, I am blessed to journey with you as Oghomwen n'Oghomwen for life.

Introduction:
Woman Trouble

*A person who knocks on the door of a wasp's nest is
asking for trouble.*

—An African proverb

Women, through no fault of their own, have always had
trouble gaining access to Jesus. The title of this book is
a direct quote from a story of one woman's trouble that appears
in various narrative permutations, allusions, and conflations in
the Gospels (Mark 14:3–9; Matt 26:6–13; Luke 7:36–50; John
12:1–7).

There are multiple manifestations of women's troubles
in the gospel narratives. In some instances, men interposed
themselves between Jesus and women as in the case of the
woman with the alabaster jar of oil (Luke 7:36–50). "What kind
of a prophet allows such a public sinner to touch him?" they
railed against Jesus. Other times, they used subtle tactics, such
as expression of surprise as in the lengthy episode of Jesus's
encounter with a female interlocutor at Jacob's well (John 4:1–
42). "Why are you talking with a woman?" his male disciples
queried without verbalizing their uncanny, furtive thought.

Why Do You Trouble This Woman?

In a more sinister situation, teachers of the law and Phari-
sees brazenly conspired to co-opt Jesus into their murderous
plan in the saga of the woman accused of adultery (John 8:1–
11). "What do you say, Jesus, to stone or not to stone?" they
yelled gleefully, fingering their lethal weapons.

Interestingly but not unsurprisingly, when women raised
their voices to demand their due, as did the Canaanite woman of
Tyre and Sidon (Matt 15:21–28), Jesus's male entourage counseled an expedient solution: "Send her away, because she keeps
shouting at us!" Compare this episode to the story of the Greeks
who requested a private audience with Jesus: "Sir, we would like
to meet Jesus." The celerity of the two male addressees and disciples was unambiguous: "Philip went and told Andrew; then
Andrew and Philip went and told Jesus" (John 12:20–22). No
questions asked.

It is no exaggeration to say that women have always had
trouble gaining access to Jesus. More accurately, male guard-
ians and gatekeepers of religion have always acted as bouncers to
exclude women from Jesus's circle of encounter. In time, women's
troubles with Jesus morphed into all kinds of bigger troubles.
What is remarkable is that Jesus stood on the side of women to
defend and protect them. "Where are your accusers?" he asked
the woman accused of adultery after shaming her attackers into
retreating, dropping their weapons, and dispersing. "Why do
you trouble this woman?" he challenged his self-righteous male
dinner host and fellow guests. Despite the prejudices and stereotypes that impugn the moral integrity and spiritual competence
of women, what truly counts is how Jesus reacted to women's
troubles. Jesus rebuked their abusers, protected them from their
attackers, and affirmed their beauty and overflowing love.

This book is partly inspired by my experience of the age-old
phenomenon of how the triad of religion, culture, and society has
troubled and continues to trouble women, and the latter's struggle to expose, resist, and overcome such trouble using various

means. In this context, this book has a salutary and positive intent. It is primarily about a valuable tool in women's quest to gain direct, personal, and intimate access to Jesus, namely, Ignatian spirituality in its concrete expression in the *Spiritual Exercises of St. Ignatius of Loyola* (born 1491, Loyola, Castile, Spain; died July 31, 1556, Rome). From this perspective, it is a book by a woman for women, although there is something in it for everyone who comes with an open mind, that is, a mind untrammeled by the myopias of sexism, stereotypes, and prejudices. What is certain is that I have written this book from a woman's perspective.

I first discovered Ignatius's *Spiritual Exercises* when I trained as a spiritual guide and companion in the famous St. Beuno's Jesuit Spirituality Centre in St. Asaph, nestled in the rolling hills of North Wales. At the time, I merely approached the encounter as a prerequisite for certification as a spiritual companion. Fortunately, when I allowed myself to be drawn into the enchanting and mystical depths of the *Exercises*, my life was transformed completely. But it was not an easy experience. Part of my struggle or trouble with the *Exercises* was its patently male-dominated penchant, stereotypes, imagery, and biases. Yet, thankfully, I persevered and gave it the benefit of the doubt as Ignatius himself counseled (see *Spiritual Exercises*, 22).[1]

For those who are new to Ignatian spirituality, the *Spiritual Exercises* is a manual or guide for prayer spread over a period of weeks. The prayers or exercises can be done under the guidance of a spiritual companion or alone, and for shorter or longer periods depending on one's circumstances. From my personal experience of "making" or "doing" the *Exercises* and from the privilege of accompanying many women on their own journey of the *Exercises*, I have reached the conviction that this is an invaluable tool for women to overcome the troubles involved in gaining access to Jesus in a manner that is spiritually personal, intimate, fulfilling, profound, and life-affirming.

Why Do You Trouble This Woman?

Over the years, I have continued to deepen my experience of the *Exercises* through practice and through learning from the experiences of a few courageous women who have dared to create their own perspectives of the *Spiritual Exercises*. As a practitioner of Ignatian spirituality, I have done the *Spiritual Exercises* in a variety of formats—long, short, and in daily living. My familiarity with and practice of Ignatian spirituality through the *Spiritual Exercises* reached a new level when I accepted the position of associate director at Marquette University's Faber Center for Ignatian spirituality in Milwaukee, Wisconsin. Joining the Faber Center team proved to be an unalloyed gift from God. Ignatian spirituality is at the core of my ministry. Along with the rest of the team, my work brought me in close contact with faculty and staff and allowed me to accompany them on their spiritual journeys and pilgrimages in formal and informal settings.

The Spiritual Exercises is a handy resource; I have relied on it to create, facilitate, experiment, and perfect a variety of spiritual programs, sessions, and activities especially for and with women. In my personal life and in my experience of journeying with women, I have discovered the priceless gem hidden in the *Spiritual Exercises*; it is easy to blow away the dust of patriarchy and androcentrism that has accumulated on the surface of the *Exercises* to reveal its awe-inspiring core, which leads women to know Jesus more intimately, to love him more dearly, and to follow him more closely. This has been my experience, and this, in part, is what I intend to share in this book.

This book is multifaceted. It is part storytelling, part journaling, part prayer, and part theology. It is neither a commentary on nor an exegesis of Ignatian spirituality in its expression in the *Spiritual Exercises*. Central to the format of this book is a story and a prayer—my story and my prayer.

This story or narrative is told in my words. It is interspersed with notes from my spiritual diary. (Ignatius left us the gift of his spiritual diary!) Pay attention to the moments of prayer in this book. Ready your heart to break into prayer from time to time. This book imitates the *Spiritual Exercises* because, like the latter, it is not a book about prayer but an exercise in prayer. My sole purpose is to invite you to discover your own story and to begin to construct your own narrative of your encounter with the Divine however you choose to imagine, embody, and contemplate this reality. I tell my story as I have lived and prayed it along with the unique grace, benefit, and privilege of accompanying many women as a spiritual companion. Their stories echo in the pages of this book. It is their story—our story.

In sharing my story of the *Spiritual Exercises* and by inviting other women to share theirs, I have both feet firmly planted on some key theological convictions that bear on my experience and understanding of Ignatian spirituality. I received a Doctor of Ministry degree (DMin) in spirituality from Catholic Theological Union, Chicago, and shortly afterward, began working on a doctoral degree in theology at Duquesne University, Pittsburgh. After the first two years of course work, I enrolled in an Ignatian spirituality program at St. Beuno's. Upon completion of this program, I successfully defended my doctoral thesis in theology at the University of Roehampton in London. My studies of spirituality and theology ignited my interest in and kindled my passion for women's troubles in religion, culture, and society. The combination of spirituality and theology enabled me to hone my feminist perceptions and convictions.

Given this theological background and trajectory, it should not surprise the reader that, as a feminist, I weave my theological perspectives into this narrative of my experience and insight on Ignatian spirituality. Authentic spirituality is rooted in sound theology.

The reverse is equally true. I have discovered that in bringing my feminist theological proclivities to bear on Ignatian spirituality, new insights and vistas have emerged. This thread of feminist theological approach runs through this book. In each chapter, I draw on my theological convictions to interrogate, deepen, and reconstruct the central themes of the *Spiritual Exercises* and Ignatian spirituality, and especially how they impact or influence the spiritual journey of women.

As I see it, God is beyond all the anthropomorphic and gender-biased attributes we have heaped upon God. God is beyond the duality of gender. Whether we are female or male, the good news is that our experience is a valid means for accessing the reality of God. Our identity and experience as women form a unique locus for encountering the Divine. As will become evident in this book, this awareness means even more to me as an African Christian woman.

I have constructed and shaped this book as a narrative of an African Christian woman, but I am not a lone voice crying out in the wilderness. A good portion of my story bears the influence of my forebears. My voice has been influenced by the lives of my remarkably strong and confident maternal grandmother, my mother, my aunties, cousins, and sisters in my lineage, as well as the women in my extended family and friends. Their ways of praying, worshipping, and celebrating their faith is intertwined with my spiritual life. From them, I have heard stories of pain and sorrow, joy and elation, and various troubles that women contend with trying to encounter the God of their lives. My preference is for telling my story as a woman and preferentially for women. I make no apology for the African flavor of this book. I can tell my story only as I am: a child of my foremothers' prayers and dreams.

The more time I spent exploring Ignatian spirituality, the more I was convinced that we cannot talk about the life and spirituality of Ignatius without acknowledging, recognizing, and celebrating the role and contribution of women, as contemporary female interpreters of Ignatian spirituality have undoubtedly demonstrated. This book fulfills all three purposes. Women have played and continue to play an integral and significant role in Ignatian spirituality. This formative and pivotal role of women in the development of Ignatius and in the emergence of Ignatian spirituality is the leitmotif of this book. This is the foundation of my belief that Ignatian spirituality and the *Spiritual Exercises* are priceless gems for women, especially when it comes to overcoming the blocks and troubles that other people place on our spiritual paths. As I demonstrate, the significance and role of women constitute perhaps one of the best-kept secrets of Ignatian spirituality. In sharing this story, I invite readers to discover this pearl, this hidden treasure of great value.

There is ample information about the women who were in direct communication with Ignatius and who helped to shape his spiritual outlook and legacy. These women were known to Ignatius as friends, donors, confidants, directees, and partners in mission. I have drawn freely from the monumental work of Hugo Rahner detailing the correspondence and dealings of Ignatius with women.[2]

It is also true that Ignatius's experience with some women was fraught with tension and misunderstanding. No doubt he had his fair share of woman trouble, albeit the fault did not lie entirely with those women. But such was the intensity of the tension that Ignatius finally decided to seek and receive from Pius III a decree, *Licet Debitum*, freeing his fledgling society from any permanent responsibility for women. Subsequently, Ignatius counseled his Jesuit confreres to proceed cautiously and prudently before accepting to serve as permanent spiritual companions or guides of lay women and nuns.

If Ignatius thought he was freeing himself and his confreres permanently from the kind of woman trouble he perceived in his time, he was mistaken; history has revealed the contrary. Ignatius may have been tempted to give up on the invaluable contribution of women to his enterprise, but women never gave up on him. The *Spiritual Exercises* display a new appeal when we consider the fact that those women as much as Ignatius have fashioned this spirituality as we know it today. In essence, the vital role of women is perhaps one of the rarely appreciated aspects of Ignatian spirituality. Women are not peripheral to the adventure of this spirituality. On the contrary, they play a key role in it. This is a nugget of wisdom to keep in mind throughout this book.

Like the women in my own life, several women have influenced and shaped Ignatian spirituality in contemporary times. Today, women across the globe have discovered and are drawing profitably from the wellspring of Ignatian spirituality. This book is inspired by and draws on the wisdom of such women, including Margaret Silf, Joyce Rupp, and Elizabeth Johnson, to name but a few.[3] Not all of them are interpreters and exponents of Ignatian spirituality, but I have found their rich perspectives on Christian spirituality to be a precious resource for plumbing the depths of Ignatian spirituality.

Two sources deserve to be singled out for mention, recognition, and appreciation. The first is the work of Katherine Dyckman, Mary Garvin, and Elizabeth Liebert. Their groundbreaking work, *The Spiritual Exercises Reclaimed: Uncovering Liberating Possibilities for Women,* did for me exactly what the title declares.[4] It opened my eyes to the limitless possibilities embedded and hidden in the *Spiritual Exercises.* The second source, from Rosemary DeJulio and Sr. Judith Lancaster, SHCJ, is their captivating exposés on the women in Ignatius's life and their incontrovertible role in the *Spiritual Exercises.*[5] These women liberated me from the flawed belief that the *Spiritual Exercises* was composed by a man and exclusively for men. By bringing women's formative influences, unique perspectives, and enduring imprint into the *Spiritual Exercises*, they opened a vast horizon of understanding and an exciting path of practical engagement with its best kept secrets and invaluable treasures. In so doing, they have inspired and empowered me to find my own voice and to set out on my own journey guided by the light of their wisdom. I owe a debt of gratitude to these women. Many of their profound and practical insights and intuitions are repeated in this book, and I have drawn abundantly and deeply on their uncommon and liberating wisdom to tell my own story.

Of course, there are also men who are exponents of Ignatian spirituality, especially in a manner that is sometimes surprisingly and refreshingly inclusive. In this sense, I have drawn freely on the insight, erudition, and wisdom of Jesuits William Barry and Robert Doherty, Kevin O'Brien, and Howard Gray.[6]

To begin this journey of discovery, in chapter 1, I invite the reader to immerse herself deeply in the memory of the many women who helped form Ignatius of Loyola and who were at the origin and foundation of Ignatian spirituality and the Society of Jesus—from Mary of Nazareth to the women who made spirited efforts to support and join Ignatius's mission to ignite the world with the fire of God's love. Rather than simply giving a straight historical account of these women, their lives, and their accomplishments, I invite the reader to pray a biographical litany of the women in Ignatius's life, those women who dedicated themselves to the Ignatian apostolic enterprise and spiritual pursuits in those early years. Through a contemplative ritual of prayer, I invite the reader to connect intimately with the lives of women at the roots of Ignatian spirituality. This reflective and contemplative connection sets the tone for what follows in this book. Also in this chapter, I invite Ignatius to tell his story in his own words, that is, his experience of woman trouble and how it nurtured, shaped, and enriched his spiritual life.

In chapter 2, I explore a familiar mantra of Ignatian spirituality, namely, finding God in all things. Using examples from the lives of women, I show that the *Exercises* and the underlying themes are not a prefabricated mold into which women's experiences can simply be plugged. Properly understood, the

Exercises are eminently flexible and adaptable; they offer a space where women can express their profound desires, explore their interior dispositions, and reflect on their external circumstances, while gently drawing on the resources of the *Exercises* and scripture to unlock their longing for freedom, depth, and wholeness.

If the core message of Ignatian spirituality is about finding God in all things, this is not a call to an impersonal, generalized quest. As women, we do not simply chase after the experience of God in fantasies and frivolities. Our experience of God is embodied in our lived realities in a unique and unrepeatable way.

In chapter 3, I explore the idea of embodiment as a key ingredient of Ignatian spirituality from the perspective of women. This chapter underscores the importance of facilitating an embodied spiritual encounter. I am keen to show that the woman who embarks on the adventure of the *Spiritual Exercises* does so holistically. No part of her life and her story is set apart. She comes as she is and brings who she is in her entirety. In this context, the role of a wise and attentive spiritual companion is not only to listen reverently and affirm this dimension respectfully but also to lead the pilgrim to connect all the dimensions of her life and to name God's actions writ large in her journey and story.

A particular and unique aspect of the idea of embodiment is the gift of the imagination. As I have experienced in my personal and ministerial life, the gift of the imagination is the key to unlocking and accessing the rich and enriching depths of Ignatian spirituality, in general, and the *Spiritual Exercises*, in particular. In this adventure, Ignatius is adamant about inviting the retreatants to deploy the gift of their imagination without borders. For women, this is a vital asset: it enables and empowers us to transcend all the limits, hindrances, and blocks that religion, culture, and society place in our paths. Without this gift of the imagination, it is impossible to enter the depths and appreciate the full measure of Ignatian spirituality. The centrality of the gift of the imagination is the main theme of chapter 4. As I point out, it is a license to explore and to enjoy the immeasurable graces of God's presence and action in our lives.

The greatest lacuna of the entire corpus of scripture, both Old and New Testaments, is the absence of women's voices. More accurately, it is the suppression of women's voices. One does not need to be a scripture scholar to reach the conclusion that scripture is a male book—written by men for men. When women's stories are told, their voices are usurped by male scribes. Yet, when it comes to spirituality as a path to encountering the divine, women's voices are nonsubstitutable. Chapter 5 makes this point precisely. Here, I look at the importance of inviting women to construct and share their personal stories and apply their imagination to contemplative prayer. Women's stories constitute a graced milieu for a divine encounter. Creating and telling our stories opens a path for us to discover sparks of the Spirit through a contemplative and holistic experience of how God is present and active in those stories.

In the sixth and final chapter, I revisit the Ignatian practice of contemplation as it appears in one of the concluding exercises in the *Spiritual Exercises*. This chapter builds on the themes explored in the preceding chapters. My main point is to show how the gift of contemplation in Ignatian spirituality enables women to see God in all things and to embark on a triple movement of awakening, awareness, and action. Awakening to God's presence in the depths of her heart is a light that expands her awareness of her beauty and giftedness. The resulting action or outcome can take many forms—praise, confidence, growth, rebirth—all of which I describe with the expression "coming home to self." A twin tool for initiating and sustaining this triple movement is discernment and the Examen, two additional unique elements of Ignatian spirituality that lie at the core of the *Spiritual Exercises*.

As noted, this book is neither a linear commentary nor an in-depth analysis of the *Spiritual Exercises*. Rather, it follows the dynamic trajectory of the *Exercises*. Several of the key themes are woven into the storyline of this book—themes including the Examen, discernment, meditation, contemplation, repetition, consolation, desolation, movements of the spirit; contemplative, imaginative, and meditative modes of prayer; the use of the senses; and the centrality of desires. These themes are highlighted prominently in the chapters depending on the perspective or the viewpoint being emphasized. Several themes of the First Week of the *Spiritual Exercises* feature in chapters 2, 4, and 6; elements of the Second Week are prominent in chapter 3; some aspects of the Third Week emerge strongly in chapter 4; and chapters 5 and 6 treat key issues in the Fourth Week.

A final word about my audience. In the *Spiritual Exercises*, Ignatius invites the retreatant to undertake an exercise that involves considering the life-choices of "three classes of persons" (*Spiritual Exercises*, 149–56). Some translations prefer "three classes of men." They face the dilemma of how to rid their souls of a particular attachment to choose and leave themselves totally open to the will of God for them. In the mind of Ignatius, each person is typical of a certain spiritual outlook on life. Using this Ignatian metaphor, I wrote this book with three classes of women in mind.

The first is the woman who is curious about the *Spiritual Exercises*. She may have heard about it or is discovering it for the first time, and she may harbor a tinge of apprehension or even suspicion about it. She is wondering whether it is for her. The second is the woman who is familiar with the Ignatian spirituality, in general, and with the *Spiritual Exercises*, in particular. This book will not be an unusual read for her. In the best tradition of Ignatian spirituality, she will find something to relish and to repeat as part of her ongoing journey of encountering and deepening her relationship with the God of her life. The third is more generally women who are engaged in the ministry of spiritual companionship and who accompany other women or men on their spiritual journeys. They, too, will recognize some important aspects of their privileged ministry in this book and profit from it for renewal and growth.

In my imagination, I have conflated all three classes of women into one that I call the woman of the *Exercises*. She may seem like a fictitious creation, but in my mind, she is not. Nor is she every woman. In various ways, she exists in the many women whom I have been privileged to accompany; she lives in my own story and narrative. As I show in this book, her story is my story too. My story is hers. Beyond fiction and imagination, by having recourse to the imagery of the woman of the *Exercises*, and as I move freely between and among the three classes of women, I hope that they will find or learn something they have not considered before—a spark, a gem, a pearl of great value to enrich their spiritual lives and expand their understanding and practice of Ignatian spirituality in their daily living.

I have allowed this woman's story to emerge and expand. Sometimes, it will be told in the first person; other times, it will be told in the second person; and often, it will be told in the third person. The storyline is the same; it is the story of the woman of the *Exercises* in its stunning diversity and intriguing variety.

For centuries, women have enriched Ignatian spirituality in their journeying and walking with St. Ignatius of Loyola. My prayer is that you will discover in this book many heartwarming ways in which his legacy requites their fidelity, sacrifice, commitment, and trust.

1

In the Beginning
Were Women

When sleeping women wake, mountains move.

—An African proverb

Women have played an integral and pivotal role in the life and spirituality of St. Ignatius of Loyola. This simple truth often lies buried beneath the weight of a regnant patriarchy in the history and traditions of the Christian church and spirituality. This chapter recalls and celebrates the memory of the many women who helped form Ignatius and as such were at the origin and foundation of Ignatian spirituality and the Society of Jesus. It would not be an exaggeration to claim that women are the pillars of Ignatian spirituality.

The compilation of *The Spiritual Exercises of Ignatius of Loyola* has existed for a few centuries. Essentially and understandably, but with notable exceptions, Jesuits have dominated the translation, interpretation, and transmission of the constitutive elements and practices of this spiritual patrimony and classic. The unintended consequence is a facile but erroneous assumption that the sources of the *Spiritual Exercises* were basically male in origin.

To undo this assumption, I invite readers to acknowledge and even immerse themselves in the distinctively feminine sources of Ignatian spirituality. While being informative for the readers, this approach will aid our understanding and deepen our comprehension of the feminine influences on the development of the *Spiritual Exercises*—from Mary of Nazareth to the women who are reading and praying with this book in the present day.

The lives of these women are intertwined with the roots of the Society of Jesus and Ignatian spirituality. I consider them our foremothers or ancestresses. This approach assumes a critical significance in the context of spirituality in Africa. In many African cultures, there is a strong belief in the continued existence of ancestors. They are often referred to as the living dead with the understanding that even in the realm of death, the bond of communion with the living remains strong, active, and significant. Many Africans believe in the existence of ancestors and call upon them for their solace and protection.

The primary purpose of making supplication to the ancestors is to ask for their protection and guidance in life. We recognize that our actions, choices, and practices have roots in the collective heritage and practices of times gone by. Our forebears continue to take interest in how we live and in what we do.

For many Christians, this practice of looking back and being conscious of our roots and origins as believers connects us with the communion of saints. The author of Hebrews acknowledged those who went before as "the great cloud of witnesses," referring to Abel, Enoch, Noah, Abraham, Isaac, Jacob, Sara, Joseph, Moses, Israelites who left Egypt, Rahab, Gideon, Barak, Samson, Jephthah, David, Samuel, and the prophets (Heb 11—12).

We are surrounded by all those women and men who have gone before us. This practice is like the practice of calling on the communion of saints when we feel the need for assistance and guidance beyond our capacity. To encounter the women at the heart and origins of Ignatian spirituality and to lay the ground-work for the key argument of this book, I begin by applying this African spiritual practice of invoking the ancestors. The advantage of this practice is that these living dead are not just names; they are memory, and they are presence; they are forebears, and they are family.

INVOKING OUR FOREMOTHERS OF THE *SPIRITUAL EXERCISES*

Let us take some time to invoke the presence and to acknowledge the gifts of the unsung women who influenced Ignatius in his spiritual growth.

Begin by relaxing all the parts of your body. Breathe in and out...breathe in and breathe out slowly...as you immerse yourself in the past. Take time to allow your mind and heart to open the hidden pages of the feminine geniuses, richness, and sources of Ignatius's spiritual foundation and formation. Continue to relax and feel the presence of all the good people in your life as well as those who have already gone beyond the veil. Allow yourself to feel the consoling manifestation of God's goodness in each person who appears in your mind's eye.

Now, allow yourself to feel this divine goodness flowing abundantly into all the parts of the world around you...into nature, the biosphere, the universe. Ignatius, too, celebrated the wonders of nature and creation in his spiritual journey. Join Ignatius and allow your mind and heart to be still as you contemplate this colorful litany of women at the foundation of the life and spirituality of Ignatius. Pause after every name or personality. Let her memory flood your imagination. Allow your heart to be surrounded by the warmth of her presence as it continues to flow through the *Spiritual Exercises of St. Ignatius*....

Why Do You Trouble This Woman?

We remember you, Dona Sanchez de Licona, Ignatius's mother. Although no record remains of your birth or death, we thank you for your strength in giving birth to and nurturing eleven children. We thank you especially for the gift of Iñigo, Ignatius....

We remember you, Maria de Garin, the blacksmith's wife, down the road from Loyola, where Ignatius was born. We remember you not only for being Ignatius's wet nurse and the maternal role you played in his life when you took him in as a child after his mother died; we remember you for nurturing Ignatius in those early years of his childhood with Christian values and spiritual consciousness.

We remember you as the one who taught Ignatius Basque words and songs and dances—the same songs and dances he would use to promote the *Spiritual Exercises* in his adult life. And through this formative path, you taught him to perceive and open his heart to God's splendor and glory in all creation....

We remember and honor you, O blessed Black Madonna of Montserrat, before whom Ignatius surrendered his life to God by placing his sword and dagger on your altar, thus beginning his journey to set the world alight with God's love....

We remember you, Mary, blessed Mother of Jesus, whose face on the painting of the Annunciation spoke profoundly to Ignatius and reminded him of the beauty of Jesus in the feminine. You are at the heart of the *Spiritual Exercises*, where Ignatius invites us to contemplate the mystery and majesty of the Incarnation using all our senses. You are the constant interlocutor in the colloquies of those who make the *Exercises*....

We remember you, Mary of Nazareth, grieving the cruel murder of your only son; the gentle woman whom, in the *Spiritual Exercises*, Ignatius invites us to contemplate as the first disciple to behold the risen Christ, the first woman to taste and receive the life-affirming and life-transforming ministry and office of consolation of the risen Christ....

We remember you all, mothers of Ignatius and mothers of the *Spiritual Exercises*. By your simple yet profoundly spiritual lives, you gave life, nurturing, and guidance to Ignatius; you formed him into the vessel and channel of God's grace that he became for generations of women and men who have prayed and continue to pray the *Spiritual Exercises*.

At the end of this contemplative exercise, I invite you to spend some time in silence allowing what you have just experienced to sink into your consciousness. Journal any thought, insight, or prayer engendered by these memories of women in the formative life of Ignatius and his spirituality; feel gratitude and thank all the women who inspired Ignatius. Imagine what each one of them meant to him and what gifts each one brought into his life and spirituality.

Now consider the women you remember from your own life. Who are the women who have shaped you into who you are today? Give thanks, too, for them.

The cardinal insight of the foregoing exercise is the awareness of and gratitude for the women who were intricately linked to the foundation, birth, and formation of Ignatius's spiritual consciousness. Ignatian spirituality is the spiritual patrimony of Christianity. As mentioned in the introduction, countless women and men have drawn from its wells of renewal and transformation in ways that even Ignatius would probably never have imagined. The simple truth is that it is not possible to think of Ignatian spirituality without honoring the contribution of women to the spiritual trajectory of Ignatius of Loyola. "The Society owes its existence to many women," wrote Rogelio Garcia-Mateo;[1] the *Spiritual Exercises* do as well.

I invite you to engage in another exercise, which brings to life the voices of some of the women who inspired Ignatius. To appreciate the depth and significance of their gift and contribution to Ignatian spirituality, it is important to give them voice and for them to speak to us imaginatively, reflectively, and contemplatively. The critical importance of women's voices in the context of Ignatian spirituality will be elucidated in later chapters.

Imagine yourself seated in the comfort of your prayer space or corner; opposite you sits one of the women in the life and spiritual journey of Ignatius sharing her story with you as she lived and now recalls it. That is the kind of presence, moment, and experience that this following exercise invites you to. It is an exercise in listening to the testimonies of the women in the life of Ignatius and in Ignatian spirituality.

Voice of Maria de Garin, Wet Nurse and Nanny to Ignatius

I was married to a blacksmith. We didn't have much, but we managed to get by. Yes, we lived down the road from the Loyola family. It was such a tragedy when Iñigo's mother died. My heart swelled with sympathy. Although my husband wasn't too happy about it, I felt compelled to take in little Iñigo as his wet nurse. I became his mom for a while.

He was a precocious and precious little bundle of energy and joy! It was such fun to watch him growing up. When I would sing to him, he would giggle and smile. I made sure that he understood who Jesus was. Oh, and I taught him the old Basque songs and dances. We had a good time together! I know little Iñigo loved the songs and dance. Did you know that years later, he would sing and dance the same Basque songs and dances to teach the *Spiritual Exercises* to his direct-ees and Jesuit companions? That was my legacy, and it continues to enchant and renew so many who walk the path of the *Spiritual Exercises*.

Pause and reflect....

Voice of Magdalena de Araoz, Who Cared for Iñigo after His Injury in the Battle of Pamplona

Magdalena is my name. Let me tell you that in his twenties, Iñigo was a reckless man. Indeed, he was a womanizer! I worried about him and prayed for him a lot, for I was married to his brother.

It was during this time in Iñigo's young life that a turn of fate brought him to stay with us in the family castle. Iñigo was wounded in battle. Both his legs were wrecked by a cannonball. He was at the point of death, or you could say he was as good as dead. It fell to me to nurse him back to health after his horrendous ordeal. I knew his wounds were not only physical. I could tell that his soul was in agony and was searching for a place of rest and contentment. Iñigo was the kind of soul who could not be confined or settle for less.

Overwhelmed by his inner restlessness, he begged me to give him books on romance and chivalry. I had a different sense of what he needed. First, I shared with him—and put it on his wall—a painting of our Lady at the Annunciation. Iñigo loved that painting! And for his literary diversion, I gave him a book on the life of Christ and another on the lives of the saints.

Daily, gradually, and consistently, as he read, I saw his boredom and depression begin to lift. Although he was still in pain from the savage surgeries with unimaginable suffering, his life was taking a different turn. His soul was in a new state. His silence became revelatory of the inner state of his soul; his solitude seemed occupied by some invisible, interior light. I knew that something profound was emerging in the depths of this young man's soul.

Iñigo was moved by what he read. As the lady of the house, I watched him and engaged with him about what he was reading.

He didn't speak much, but through the pain of his suffering, I saw a change taking place in him.

When he was well enough, he departed for a popular pilgrimage place. That was when I knew that God had stirred up something special in his soul that would become a gift to the world.

At the place of pilgrimage, something dramatic happened; Iñigo decided to leave his sword at the statue of Our Lady of Montserrat, the Black Madonna. That was the first of many conversions that he would experience on his lifelong pilgrimage. He gave up everything freely and decided to make up for the sins of his past. Not to be outdone, he went a little far by wearing disheveled hair; he lived in a cave, and some speculated that he was perhaps even becoming suicidal. He fasted. He became ill. He had to be taken care of.

Yes indeed, this was a man in search of himself, or rather, I should say, God was in search of Iñigo.

Pause and reflect....

Voice of Inez Pascual, Iñigo's First Partner in Mission

I am Inez Pascual, the first woman to share Iñigo de Loyola's spiritual experience soon after he began the journey of his conversion with God. I recall the experience vividly, almost like it happened yesterday. It was on the Feast of the Annunciation in 1522, almost a year after his horrendous injury in the Battle of Pamplona. That date has stuck in my mind!

At the time, the man who would become St. Ignatius of Loyola was quite a sight to behold. Attired in the sackcloth of the wannabe holy men of his day, he was limping laboriously as he eased his way down from Mount Montserrat through the valley to Manresa. It didn't take long, after I met him, for God's plan for his life to become intertwined with mine and with the lives of the women of Manresa who affiliated with him. We regarded ourselves as the Iñigas.

I was a normal housewife; I was married and had my first son, Juan. Then, I lost my husband, Juan Sagrista, and became a widow. I got married a second time to Bernardino Pascual, who lived in Barcelona. This marriage also ended sooner than I had imagined. I had no child with him but received a substantial inheritance. So, you see, I then had a house and a shop near the church of Santa Maria del Mar in Barcelona. I also owned a home in Manresa. Many years later, my son had this to say about my relationship with Ignatius:

> My mother was coming back from a visit to the Holy House of Our Lady of Montserrat with two of her kinsmen, named Juan Torres and Miguel Canyelles, and three women, Paula Amigant, Catalina Molins, and the matron of the hospital, Jeronima Claver, who were all widows. When they reached the hermitage of the Holy Apostles, which is situated a little below the monastery, she met a young man dressed as a pilgrim, of low stature, with a pale face and reddish hair, whose manner was so grave and modest that he hardly raised his eyes from the ground; and he limped with the right foot. The man asked my mother if there was in the neighborhood a hospice in which he might lodge for a few days. Being struck by the noble yet friendly air of the pilgrim, she looked at him more closely and felt moved to piety and devotion. She answered that the nearest hospice was three miles away and that she herself was going thither and, if he were willing, she would be of use and service to him, to the best of her ability. The pilgrim was pleased with my mother's offer and decided to follow her.[2]

Pause and reflect....

Why Do You Trouble This Woman?

Voice of Isabel Roser, Iñigo's First Benefactress

You can call me Isabel. I came to know Ignatius when he was teaching catechism to children in the streets of Barcelona. When I first met him, he was still full of the verve and fervor of a pilgrim whose sole focus was to make the perilous trip to Jerusalem. There was something different about him, though. He was simple and modest yet deeply spiritual and insightful. He talked little but left a lasting imprint on your soul. There was such a powerful aura around him that always left you captivated. So, I befriended him, and my husband, a wealthy merchant, enabled me to provide financial resources to support Ignatius. Indeed, because I was part of the nobility, my influence was significant for him. I was able to motivate others in my circle to assist him with the pursuit of his dreams.

Several years later, after the death of my beloved husband, I began to consider life in the convent. It wasn't clear how I could do it, but I decided to travel to Rome to join Ignatius in his work. Once begun, the work was so fulfilling; I realized that I had discovered a second vocation. God was calling me to something deeper, just as I believed God was doing in Ignatius's life. In fact, his passion had lit a fire in my soul to work for the good of souls and the greater glory of God, as Ignatius himself used to tell us.

Two other women and I were so committed to the work that we petitioned the pope to allow us to take vows under the guidance of Ignatius. Much to our delight, the pope obliged us, but Ignatius was not so enthusiastic. Lucrezia di Bradine, Francisca Cruyllas, and I were thrilled to take vows. As I said, perhaps Ignatius was not too excited by our unexpected experiment, but we felt called. He had touched our souls with his passion, but things didn't work out as we had hoped.

A short while later, Ignatius asked the pope to dispense us from our vows. It was a sad and painful breakup, and I then became estranged from Ignatius for several years. I returned to Barcelona dejected and angry. Thankfully, years later, we reconciled.

In the end, I entered a convent, since my heart still desired to serve God. Once I was smitten by the transformative power of Ignatius's spiritual depth, I was never the same.[3]

Pause and reflect....

Voice of Princess Juana of Spain, the First Jesuitess

I am the famous Juana, and I can comfortably claim to be the only woman who became a Jesuit, or rather, a Jesuitess. I will spare you the details because it is a long story, but let me give you the gist, enough for you to know what Ignatius meant for me and what I meant for him.

I was born Infanta, second daughter of Isabella of Portugal and Charles V of Spain. I lost my mother when I was only four. It fell to Leonor Mascareñas, a friend of my mother's, to raise me as her own daughter. My father supervised my upbringing from afar.

Interestingly, these women knew of Ignatius of Loyola. There was a Jesuit, Fr. Araoz, I believe was his name, who preached in the court of the king. When I was sixteen, Fr. Araoz was once again called to preach to the court. He wasn't the only Jesuit to preach in the king's court. There was also the famous Fr. Francis Borgia. I assume the Jesuits thought it wise to take me through the *Spiritual Exercises* since I was perceived to be the apparent consort of my sickly bridegroom, John Emanuel.

I was fortunate to have Fr. Borgia as my spiritual director. When I was seventeen, John and I were married. Fr. Borgia came to Lisbon and to the royal court in 1553. Honestly, I did what I could to bring the entire court into complete alignment with the presence of Jesus Christ and the Jesuits. Sadly, my infirm husband passed away, and eighteen days later, I bore him a son, the future King Sebastian.

Things happened rather quickly. A few months later, my father, the emperor, appointed me as regent in Spain, since my brother Philip would be absent because of his marriage to Mary Tudor. So, at age nineteen, I became the regent of Spain, and I held that position for five years. It was fun to be in charge. I loved being the boss in a court packed with men jostling for influence and aspiring to various positions of importance. Yet deep in my soul, there was a yearning, an aching for something more than any power or authority could assuage. It had something to do with the Ignatian way.

I turned to Fr. Borgia for spiritual direction and guidance in how to rule. Unbeknown to me, that deep longing was for me to become a Jesuit. My trusted confidantes, Frs. Borgia and Araoz, facilitated the process and wrote to Ignatius to tell him of my desire. Thus began a fascinating and lively correspondence with Ignatius of Loyola. In the end, after many consultations with other Jesuits, Ignatius allowed me to take vows as a scholastic in the Society of Jesus. True to character, Ignatius imposed strict conditions: I was to tell nobody of this development or change my lifestyle in any way. Remarriage was ruled out. After all, I was a Jesuit scholastic! Under the pseudonym of Mateo Sánchez, I began my life as a vowed member of the Jesuits. The rest, as they say, is history.

Pause and reflect....

This sampling of testimonies of women in the life of Ignatius is incomplete. We will encounter more later. At every turn in Ignatius's life were women who found inspiration in his spiritual pilgrimage and walked part of it with him by working with him as collaborators, providing the financial means for him to realize his mission, or both.

Understandably, not all of them have been given voice to tell their stories; their stories have been filtered through many narratives, authored by historians and interpreters of Ignatian spirituality, the vast majority of whom were men.

My discovery of the role of women in the foundation and formation of Ignatius, his *Spiritual Exercises*, and Ignatian spirituality, in general, is the fruit of a long journey. Perhaps like you, I have always found the language of Ignatian spirituality patently androcentric and militaristic, the former on account of the theology of his day and the latter a fruit of his experience as a courtier. In my many journeys in spirituality, I never imagined that women were part of the beginnings of the *Exercises* and Ignatian spirituality. Now, however, it is a different story. I am consoled knowing that this spirituality was influenced and formed by women in so many ways. I have heard some Jesuits say that "Mary, our blessed Mother, actually gave the *Spiritual Exercises* to Ignatius." If they are right, then women are at the heart and foundation of the *Spiritual Exercises.* That is the rationale and the narrative of this book.

What would Ignatius make of all this talk about women in his life and in the foundation and formation of the *Spiritual Exercises* and Ignatian spirituality? We could speculate, but we can also draw from his insight to construct his narrative. Just like the women in the foregoing paragraphs, we can also give him a voice to tell his story and offer his perspective. Perhaps he would rather not recall uncomfortable memories of his experience of women's troubles in his life. Maybe not, but in my own contemplative reconstruction, here is what I imagine Ignatius saying.

VOICE OF IGNATIUS

This is not another autobiography. Far from it. Rather than repeat everything you have just read, I will simply tell you about the woman who most influenced me, the woman who inspired the love of her son in me. As you know from what you have read so far, I experienced the presence of many women in my life, but it was Mary, our blessed Mother, who walked with me in the ups and downs of my life. Have you noticed that I created the apocryphal narrative in the *Spiritual Exercises* that the risen Christ appeared to Mary before anybody else? [*Spiritual Exercises*, 218–25]. Interestingly, this claim has never been challenged, questioned, or condemned as unorthodox or heretical.

You know, too, that I asked for a book to read to dissipate my boredom during my convalescence in the family castle of Loyola and that the kindly and maternal Magdalena gave me the only kind of books she would tolerate in the house. Everything she said above is correct. She knew of my vanity, love for women, and reckless living, but she would not countenance any of that in the house. She must have known that my soul was fashioned for bigger and greater things for God and for the world.

But let me tell you, Magdalena was a gorgeous woman! Whenever I looked into her eyes, I saw a resemblance to the painting of our blessed Mother that hung on the wall of my room. I felt her determined feminine power and presence as she came into my room and gave me those two books that would change my life for good. She practically commanded me with just one word: Read!

But I need to share a bigger piece of my story with you so that you can understand how deeply women like Magdalena influenced me. You know me as Ignatius of Loyola, but I was born Iñigo, the eleventh child of my mother. Bearing eleven children was no mean feat in those days of elevated infant and maternal mortality. My mother succumbed to the latter when I was a child.

It fell to Maria de Garin and the blacksmith family to raise me as she rightly described above. She was truly the mother of my dreams; I could never have become the Ignatius whom the world knows and celebrates today without Maria. She was modest when she said that she had taught me Basque words, songs, and dance; there was so much more that she gave me. She nurtured my mind, body, and soul to begin, albeit inchoately, to listen, see, and sense God's glory and presence in all people and in all things. Does this remind you of the *Spiritual Exercises*? Of finding God in all things? I am sure it does.

Of course, I wasn't born a saint. By now, everybody has heard about my embarrassing past pursuits of vanities of the world until a cannonball put paid to my worldly ambitions and confined me to bed as an invalid. You can imagine the boredom and loneliness that racked my mind and soul. The only consolation—wait for it—was to daydream about an imaginary lady whom I would serve once I regained the use of my crippled legs. As things would have it, I needed more than just my imagination to fuel that fantasy. Surely there must be some chivalrous and romantic novels to feed my fancy. Oh dear, was I mistaken! I was in the wrong house and in the wrong company. My sister-in-law, Magdalena, wouldn't have any of my craving for knight-in-shining-armor tales of amorous adventures and chivalrous escapades. She gave me what she had and what in her feminine genius she intuited I needed.

So, there I was reading about the life of some long-dead Galilean Jew and his enchanted cohorts of imitators they called saints. Little did I know that I was in for an emotional roller-coaster ride. The effect of the forced *lectio* was magical, entrancing, and intriguing. When I read about the exploits of the sometimes crazy and overzealous imitators of Jesus and mused about how I too could imitate and even outdo them, I was transported to an outer galaxy of exhilarating feelings. Then, the thoughts of my noble lady waiting for her knight on a white charger would set in and my feelings would soar ever more wildly into the galaxies. I cannot begin to tell you how it felt. It was dizzying, even as I recall it now after many centuries.

Why Do You Trouble This Woman?

Then something happened. I noticed that my feelings had a weird pattern. Even though the thought of imitating Jesus and that of serving my noble lady transported me into psychological ecstasy, the latter came crashing down while the former soared even higher. Musings about imitating Jesus brought me inner joy, contentment, and peace; the opposite left me empty, dry, and deflated. That was when it hit me: the path of Christ causes consolation while the path of vanity triggers desolation, as we will explore later.

Aha! During one of those turbulent nights, I had a vision, one that carried a clear message. I saw our blessed Mother carrying the baby Jesus in her arms. I saw the Madonna and child. This brought me so much lasting inner peace and joy. I would return to the experience over and over, and the consolation would be greater each time. Little did I realize that I was being formed to become more and more attuned to the beauty and goodness of our blessed Mother and her son.

My life was taking a turn toward something more profound. I even began to see my nascent spiritual life in colors— red for Jesus, blue for Mary—and to recite this spiritual color coding like a mantra. My heart was filled with delight. All I wanted to do was to speak about God's presence and goodness to everyone in my family. While some of them thought I was crazy, the ever-astute Magdalena was quietly impressed to see what I was becoming, though she was too modest to take credit for what she had inspired in me.

My whole family could see the changes happening in me. I was growing into my own self as God created me to be in truth, beauty, and goodness. A new path was unfolding before me, and I was anxious to set out into the uncharted road of God's love and goodness in my life. Everything seemed right. I wanted to walk the path of Jesus in his far-off native Jerusalem. Even the stars at night seemed propitiously aligned with my dreams. Every night, I would go outside and watch the stars and they would all shine brightly and smile warmly on my parched soul and move me to deep prayer and a deep desire to give my all in service to my God.

My desire to set out on a pilgrimage of service to Jesus rattled even my unflappable older brother. He tried everything he could to dissuade me, including showing me the riches and wealth of my family estate. "This is yours, Iñigo," he would remind me. "It's all yours—such riches and wealth. You belong here. The hope and future of generations of Loyola rest on you, in this place. Don't let us down for the futility of dreams and fantasies."

I loved my family, but my family—thanks to Maria and Magdalena—had opened my heart and soul to a deeper love of our blessed Lady and her son, Jesus. I owed them everything. But let me muse a little more about Magdalena's intuition in giving me those books about the life of Christ and the lives of saints. This is not an empty musing. Imagine if she had not had the perspicacity to offer me those books. Imagine if I had not had that moment in my life of discovering the new tales of Christian living and had simply persisted in my craving for tales of chivalry and amorous exploits. Imagine if Magdalena had bought into my wiles and guiles and given me a different genre of reading material to assuage my gnawing boredom and while away the time.

Sometimes when I recall those moments, I wonder whether Jesuits realize the singular importance of Magdalena in my life and in the foundation of the Society of Jesus. Let me say this: the Society of Jesus owes Magdalena a debt of gratitude. Perhaps the fitting way to repay this debt is to pay attention to and honor the pivotal role that women continue to play in the development of the *Spiritual Exercises*. Those women were really the pillars and shoulders that I needed to prop myself up from my bed of illusion to see all things new in Christ. I had not realized it myself at the time, something that I deeply regret.

In the cultural framework and context of patriarchy and sexism of my day, such a realization was slow. Perhaps I got too embroiled in sorting out my troubles with the women who desperately wanted to be part of my nascent enterprise. My point is that women were an integral part of my spiritual upbringing, consciousness, and development. This is a gospel truth that my Jesuit descendants must never forget.

Back to my story. It was time to leave the family home after I had been nursed back to health. My brother's pleas fell on deaf ears. I left my home early one morning in March 1522, burning with a passion to make my first stop at the shrine of Our Lady of Aranzazu up the hill in Loyola. Such was my passion and eagerness to get there that I refused all help and assistance offered by my brother. I had to do this alone—with the help of Mary and Jesus.

At that time in my life, you could say that I had a somewhat fanatical love for Mary. Maybe I had unconsciously transferred my passion for my fantasy lady to my love and zeal for our Lady and her son. This much I know: I wanted to distinguish myself in their service. So strong was this desire that once when I encountered a man who seemed to disparage our Lady, a fierce desire seized me to run after him and stab him to death. If you are reading this story today, it is because God saved me from the folly of committing first-degree murder in the name of protecting the virginal conception of our Lady. Or was it a mule that saved the day? So be it.

My first journeys were solitary. I was alone, responding to this new call to follow Jesus more closely. It was a tough and enlightening experience. But the lessons were not lost on me. God was teaching me through so many means—people, events, and places—about the journeys of the soul. And I was learning things I could never have learned from any book. That is the power and uniqueness of the *Spiritual Exercises*; you pray rather than read them.

I continued my journey with a deep desire to spend the night and vigil at the top of Mount Montserrat. I had brought with me some old clothes and sackcloth and was ready to change from my rich and lovely clothes into some that were more modest. I was prepared to begin my new life, reflected in everything that was part of me: my clothing, my food, my body—everything in me was calling for a change. And so, I left my sword on the altar of Our Lady of Montserrat. This gesture was a symbol of my new life. No longer would I be fighting as a knight under the auspices of some worldly royal court. I would be a foot soldier for Christ, armed with my life of poverty, simplicity, and service to humanity. In short, the world would become my house, as one of my trusted aides, Jerónimo Nadal (1507–80), would later describe the essence of the Jesuit missionary spirit.

The gesture of renunciation filled me with love and joy as I felt the presence of Mary affirming my new life. The only unfortunate part of this experience was what happened to the man to whom I gave my rich clothes. He was mistaken for a thief, caught, and harassed. Thank God that he found me and that I could attest to his innocence.

Not only did I give up my dagger, sword, and clothes; I added my horse to boot. My transformation from a knight to a pilgrim was complete. A new path was unfolding before me. In those early days, I was developing a habit of taking notes of any spiritual insights—what caught my attention and how I felt about it. In that way, I was guided to understand what God was doing in my life.

It was at this time that I met Inez Pasqual and some other friends who were with her. As she narrated above, they were very hospitable to me. They, too, were walking down the hill from the retreat at the Benedictine monastery and Our Lady of Montserrat, where I had just spent the night in front of the Black Madonna.

As we walked and compared notes about what was happening to us spiritually, we struck up a partnership that was to be an important part of my life and ministry. In fact, she and the women in Manresa helped me with the formation of the *Spiritual Exercises*. You could say that I practiced and prayed the *Exercises* with them. Our spiritual paths were so bound together and mutually enriching that they even called themselves Iñigas, the feminine form of Iñigo, after my name.

Through them, I learned so many things. Their feminine way of perceiving the Spirit alive and active in the world was a gift to me. Their perceptions provided me insights so deep that I couldn't have become your Ignatius of Loyola without them. In fact, there would have been no Society of Jesus without the formation I received from these women and so many other women. They were deeply spiritual women who formed me. But they have already told their stories. I might simply add that they are true.

While I was at the hospice in Manresa, where I was provided with accommodation, I let my hair grow. My nails became long and unkempt. I fasted, believing this was the way to sanctity. I cut the scary image of a Neanderthal man. Worse still, my feelings swung wildly between joy and sorrow, exhilaration and depression.

Then one day, something special happened. I had an encounter with an older woman who was renowned for her spiritual life. I had heard that even the king of Spain consulted her regarding spiritual matters. One day, she approached me and said, "Would that the Lord Jesus might appear to you some day." I found her words confusing and at first took them to be a literal sort of prophecy about the Lord appearing to me. Why me? I wondered. Yet her words gave me delight as I imagined Jesus appearing to me.

Although our encounter was fleeting, I never forgot her because her prophecy was fulfilled to the letter in my later years. As I tried to show in the *Spiritual Exercises*, Jesus appeared to me multiple times. That little old lady spoke words that described the foundation and goal of the *Spiritual Exercises* as a way of experiencing the multiple channels and means by which God encounters and appears to us.

Despite the psychological turbulence and the tension that threatened to derail my spiritual journey on so many occasions, the words of the wise old woman proved to be a solid anchor. I had hope and delight in meeting Jesus, and the experience brought me consolation and joy. The thought of knowing that Jesus was with me and that my life would be spent following and serving him was an inexhaustible font of joy and peace. I couldn't have wished for more!

A GUIDED MEDITATION

I invite readers to do an exercise recollecting and praying with the story of Ignatius.

Find a comfortable place and assume a comfortable posture. Take a few deep breaths. Allow all your senses to become aligned with and attuned to your surroundings and environment....

Recall the abridged story of Ignatius in his own words. Which aspects of his story resonate with yours? Then listen to the words of the wise old woman reassuring you as she did Ignatius that Jesus will appear to you....

Imagine Jesus sitting in front of you and speaking to you. Feel the presence of his Spirit. Hear his comforting words...and begin to address God according to your emotions and feelings. Speak the language of your heart to God as one friend would to another. Be at peace with yourself and with your God.

2

Finding God in All Things

A fully grown-up tree cannot be bent into a walking stick.

—An African proverb

The primary focus of this book originates in the insight that rather than being strange bedfellows, the *Spiritual Exercises* and women's spirituality are aligned and that women can bring an understanding of the former and experience its richness for their lives in creative, transformative, and life-affirming ways.

It is easy to see the reason for this relationship. Judging from the themes I developed in chapter 1, the relationship between Ignatius and women was formative for his life and the spirituality that developed from his life. In this chapter, I offer illustrations of the richness of Ignatian spirituality for women by considering some of its familiar themes.

As mentioned in the introduction and in chapter 1, women have noticed and commented on the patriarchal and androcentric penchant of the *Spiritual Exercises*. It is a familiar observation that doubles as a poignant critique in the context of feminist theology. I recall an incident with a friend, who signed up for an eight-day Ignatian retreat. Unsurprisingly, she stopped before the retreat concluded. Her decision made sense; she just could not cope with the language and the choice of scriptures that spoke nothing to her personal and present experiences as a woman. Her reaction would be perfectly understandable to anybody familiar with the *Spiritual Exercises*. Yet, as I note throughout this book, besides this linguistic and scriptural masculinity, androcentrism, and militarism, there are other influences—those of women—in the *Exercises*. The perspective opens a fresh, new doorway to the heart of Ignatian spirituality.

Think, for example, about the beauty of seeing God in all things or using your imagination in prayer to smell, taste, feel, touch, see. I consider these spiritual practices inspired by the *Spiritual Exercises* as predominantly feminine touches of Ignatian spirituality.

In the imaginative space of the *Exercises*, it is even permissible to imagine Jesus as a woman companion and to see yourself sitting and chatting with God. Thus, nothing stops us as women from looking beyond the language and bringing our present-day experiences to enrich and transform a sixteenth-century prayer manual. The *Spiritual Exercises* can be truly transformative and fulfilling for women, but on the face of it, this is not self-evident.

Why are so many people ignorant of the role women played in the life of Iñigo and Ignatius of Loyola? Such ignorance can breed resentment and create distance between women and the *Exercises*. I believe this has been a common feature in women's engagement with the *Exercises* over many years. I hold the unshakable conviction that Ignatius could never have accomplished what he did and become the person he was without women. I have made a case for this position in the preceding chapter.

Being raised by a woman; surrounded by women who helped him, psychologically and spiritually, in his developmental years; and encouraged by women who were there allowing him to "practice" his spiritual skills were critical aspects that shaped Ignatius's life. In his time, he inspired many women and was inspired by many women as well.

Based on what I noted in the preceding chapter, Ignatius's experience with women was anything but smooth and uncomplicated. From early on, his relationship with some women was fraught and tense. He admitted some into his fledgling order grudgingly and readily facilitated their dismissal shortly afterward. Understandably, Ignatius was a man of his times and, accordingly, ill-prepared to deal with strong, confident, and determined women who were convinced of their call to lead lives of spiritual virtue. Nevertheless, the complicated relationship and dealings with women form part of the enduring legacy of Ignatian spirituality and its success over the centuries in helping women and men to find God in all things.

WOMEN FINDING GOD IN ALL THINGS

The motto "to find God in all things" encapsulates a cardinal tenet of Ignatian spirituality and resonates, I believe, with the spiritual core of women's experience. By the very nature of their availability for the well-being of others and their inclusive hospitality, many women naturally find God in all things. But what does this mean in relation to the *Spiritual Exercises*?

The first thing to note is women's ability to perceive, think, and act holistically. Women can draw insights from the experience of handling many situations at the same time and, in the process, derive meaning and sense for their lives.

A woman's ability to multitask can also be a spiritual power. Think of a career woman with a full-time job who is making dinner, cleaning her house, answering her many text messages, putting herself together to arrive on time at work—to say nothing of listening to family quarrels and the happenings of the day. It is no mean feat by any standard.

Or consider a single woman who is very involved in her community, even as she keeps up with a very demanding career and profession. Perhaps also a single mother who has two or three children—getting them to school on time while keeping up with the demands of her career and her struggles to keep herself together in the many challenges of her life.

In all these instances, each woman is making the best out of every situation to derive meaning and purpose for her life and the lives of others. In fact, consciously or unconsciously, in all her multiple commitments and engagements, she is being present to the God whom her heart desires in her every experience. She is not simply an accomplished multitasker. At the heart of her activities lies a deep desire, yearning, and passion for the God who is present in all things and who ceaselessly nudges her on. The miracle here is not the physical or psychological manifestation of strength, but a spiritual connection with interior depth and energy. She keeps hope alive while trusting that the God who is present to her will manifest the Divine in one way or the other. Her chores do not becloud her desires, and her engagements do not dim her passion for the God of her life.

Consider, for example, a woman who struggles incessantly to achieve spiritual balance and consistency, to love each person in her family, to maintain integrity of mind, heart and spirit, and to remain attuned to the present of the Divine in it all.

I will call her Meg, a mother of two children. Her husband filed for divorce and left her in the lurch. Gone was the salary he had brought home. She had no idea just how she was going to cope with her life and the avalanche of new responsibilities for which she was unprepared. Every month, she wondered how she would pay the bills. Every month, she held her breath, wondering how she would make it. Yet somehow she confessed to having a profound connection with God as her source, her provider. This connection was a blend of intimacy, trust, confidence, and hope.

No matter the challenges and circumstances of the times, Meg could always count on a special presence that exuded divinity. She could find God in the middle of things. She told me that, at one point, things had improved and that she no longer found herself depending on God in quite the same way. It was surprising to hear her say, "Well, now that things are better, I do miss that sense...that special sense of intimacy and closeness I had with God. It isn't the same now." It may not be the same, but God is faithful and promises to be with us without fail. Finding God in all things also means that God is finding us in all things, in all spaces, at all times.

A woman practicing Ignatian spirituality can become more aware of how God is present in the myriad of challenges in her life. Based on my experience of accompanying many women on their journey of the *Spiritual Exercises*, I am convinced that women can receive the grace of becoming more attentive to the God who is present in all their doings. For the woman of the *Exercises*, this grace is a reminder that her life is touched by divine love.

The quest to find God in all things is an invitation to look at key moments and aspects of the *Spiritual Exercises* more closely and creatively. Consider, for example, Ignatius's reading of sin and sinfulness. When Ignatius invites the retreatant to pray for the grace of a "healthy sense of shame" in the First Week of the *Spiritual Exercises*, one must ask, What does a healthy sense of shame mean for a woman? In the context I am familiar with, this is a challenging question for any woman. If poorly handled in the context of spiritual accompaniment, it can further reinforce stereotypes and multiple forms of gender-based distortions of the identity and integrity of women. For so many women who have experienced abuse in the church or in their families, or who have been socialized to develop a negative image of themselves as women, often perpetrated by a perverse catechetics that promotes the hideous notion of women as the root of all evil, any sense of shame could pile up more psychological and spiritual burdens on them.

Rather than imply repentance for sins visited on her by her culture, church, and society, in the context of the *Spiritual Exercises*, praying for the grace of a healthy sense of shame would involve standing up for herself and resisting the imposition of negative cultural, religious, or societal prescriptions on her. It is a sense of recognizing oneself as created in the image and likeness of God rather than being defined by forms engendered by ecclesial patriarchy and social gender typecasting. This sense would include a deep pride in her body and her giftedness as a woman. Such attitudes, and in fact the joy of being born a woman, make not only for a healthy sense of shame but also for a confident sense of self.

If we plumb the depths and purpose of the *Spiritual Exercises*, we discover that it can be truly liberating for women. Another transformative dynamic of the *Exercises* is the direct encounter between the retreatant and her God (*Spiritual Exercises*, 15). This space of unmediated encounter can be emancipating for women, especially because of the many crippling and disempowering expectations and constructs of women's lives engineered by others. It is a space that invites and allows her to tell her truth.

Consider the example of someone I will call Kate, who had been married for five years. She had never liked cooking. Nevertheless, she kept pretending to be a cook to please her husband. She had been raised to believe that it was the role of the dutiful wife to cook dinners every evening.

One day, however, she had really had enough. She let it all out. She yelled at her husband, "Every day, I cook with anger and resentment! I'm not your maid!" Her husband was stunned. Up to that moment, he had never understood why Kate was always angry after cooking and when she served him his meals. Kate told Dan (not his real name) that her in-laws kept making her feel that she could never marry her husband if she was not going to be serving him. Serving him included making him dinner every night. Serving him meant doing his laundry. Serving him meant being at his beck and call whenever he wanted something.

It was at this breaking point that Kate realized that she was not happy to be so subservient to any man. She became aware that she could not carry out these implicit wishes and demands anymore and certainly not in a long-term marriage. She had gone on retreat and had shared with her spiritual companion that she was very unhappy in her marriage. Back home, in a moment of truth, she poured out all her frustrations to her husband. Because he had been brought up with these unspoken expectations, it had never occurred to him to question these cultural norms. He was shocked and humbled by his beloved wife's explosion.

Stepping back, Kate herself was shocked at her truth-telling experience. Yet it was precisely at that moment that she felt the invitation of the *Spiritual Exercises* to a healthy sense of shame, a space where she could find the light and courage to see the God of her life and discover a presence of love and freedom, trust and transformation. This moment of discovery and encounter changed her life and her husband's life. Such is the power of finding God in all things for women who come to the *Spiritual Exercises* with a deep yearning and passion for the God of their lives.

The story did not end there. Her experience of finding God in all things had a practical effect on her life. Kate had found that this practice of cooking for her husband and constantly being called on to fulfill his every whim had been diminishing her. Once her initial irritations were spoken and she could discover the deeper presence, meaning, and purposes of God for her life, Kate regained her inner balance and spoke in a calmer tone: "Dan, we both have full-time jobs. We would both be helped by having a conversation about how we might do things differently."

Because she was operating from a place of depth, Kate could engage her husband in serious truth telling regarding their lives together. She expressed her wish that he would join her in the kitchen when they came back from work instead of watching TV or gossiping with his friends on the phone. Kate imagined that they could do many things together as a couple. Finding God in all things is a contagious spiritual experience. Far from being proprietary, it is communal. Women who discover this spiritual nugget of wisdom in their lives readily spread it to all those around them, as Kate did with Dan.

FINDING THE GIFTS AND FRUITS OF THE SPIRIT

Through this example of Kate and Dan's marriage, we can see what it means to speak in terms that Ignatius uses to assist us in discerning how God is working in us and our lives—in finding God in all things. There are two words that need to be explored so we can understand how God's presence is manifested in the concrete circumstances of our lives—consolation and desolation. Ignatius uses these terms to assist us in reflecting on our feelings and emotions and how they function as pointers both to our interior dispositions and to the state of our being with God.

Once Kate expressed her truths to Dan, she felt a lightness of heart, and after Dan got over his initial shock, he too felt some relief. Perhaps both had been experiencing desolation before they came to the moment of truth telling. In practical and concrete ways, Kate's experience was an illustration of God's healing and consoling presence in her ordinary experience. Through an encounter of intimacy with God, she experienced God loving her and filling her soul with life.

It was also an empowering experience. She was not going to continue to accept societal norms that a woman should be subservient to her partner as a matter of divine mandate. Ignatian spirituality is anything but a facile confirmation of stock biases and prejudices. Rather, it is an invitation to look more deeply into where we as women can identify footprints of God in our lives and where we are becoming more alive as a result of this spiritual renewal process. I have chosen the word *footprints* to illustrate the importance of paying attention, in Ignatian spirituality, to all aspects of a person's life in a holistic and intentional manner. I will elaborate on this point in later chapters dealing with the gift of imagination and the notion of embodiment.

Embarking on the adventure of Ignatian spirituality is an invitation to women to reflect more deeply on their life experiences. To find God in all things, they must be intentionally attentive. Like Kate, women who are saddled and burdened with socially constructed gender expectations and tasks can hardly find the time to reflect on their days. Culturally, there is little encouragement for women to take time for personal reflection. Part of this reality is shaped by the demands of bringing in a paycheck. Also, part of this reality is caused by the rush and demands of those around her and, especially, family members— taking care of parents, tending to children, being present to her spouse. Appropriately, taking time for herself is a treasure that is often hidden in the field. Even taking the time to identify the treasure of solitude and reflection is not immediately available to many women.

Fortunately, through the *Spiritual Exercises*, the woman of the *Exercises* is invited to become more attentive and present to who she is and how she functions as a person. The *Exercises* invites her to be more attuned to her immediate surroundings and environment, situation, and context by reflecting on her realities. That may entail taking time for and practicing some silence in her daily prayer style. In this way, the woman would become more present to the God who desires to guide her into a deeper relationship.

As a woman, she can now discern where God is active and present and bringing her to life, and alternatively, where the negative and contrary spirit—sometimes disguised as the good spirit—can lead her to pain and distress. She can deepen and grow from the practice of contemplation, and she can benefit from learning to consider her affective responses, such as Kate learned.

Through the authenticity of her feelings, she can recognize where God is present and life-giving. Kate had never been happy simply fulfilling societal expectations and handling domestic chores. Things began to change when she was able to pay attention to her reactions and feelings and was willing to recognize them as pointers to a place of desolation. Her experience of the *Exercises* opened her eyes to what was going on in her life, and it empowered her to discern where God was calling her—to a place of growth, freedom, and flourishing. As mentioned, the art and act of paying attention to interior movements is an important dimension of Ignatian spirituality that Ignatius established quite early in his spiritual trajectory.

As we saw in chapter 1, Ignatius was able to discern God in all things as he paid close attention to God inviting him to be more of who he could be for God and others. Like Ignatius, Kate became more aware of who she could be for her family. Indeed, if she could experience cooking as an opportunity to be with her husband by cooking together, she was then enabled to challenge her husband to become part of this activity.

In the end, Dan was grateful to be part of it. He discovered that he even liked cooking and being the chef. Both spent intimate moments cutting onions, blending tomatoes, and grilling chicken. God became more present in their marriage not through a flashing, blinding revelation, but in the ordinary process of paying attention to what was going on inside and how it was shaping what was going on outside and around them.

Kate began to feel loved and supported by her husband. Their marriage and bond grew stronger as they spent more time together doing grocery shopping, making lists, and creating menus for their meals. Kate found the "God in all things" in her cooking when her husband was part of it. She experienced the consolation of God in the life-giving experience of lovingly doing the work with her husband as equals, as partners.

The important lesson here is that for the woman of the *Exercises*, finding God in all things does not translate into becoming subservient and accepting oppressive situations. As noted above, for many women, engaging in the *Exercises* presents them with a beckoning door into self-reflection and into a new life with the one who loves us. For the woman of the *Exercises*, finding God in all things can be an invitation to finding her best self and coming home to that self with confidence and joy. It could mean finding and reveling in the fruits of the Spirit or, as Ignatius put it, experiencing "greater interior motions and spiritual relish" (*Spiritual Exercises*, 227). In her times of reflection, she can ask herself, *Just where are the fruits of the Spirit in this experience?* By intentionally paying attention to the daily movements in her heart, her life experiences begin to point her to the gifts and fruits of the Spirit.

INTENTIONAL ATTENTIVENESS

In the preceding section, I mentioned the experience of relishing the fruits of the Spirit. I do not mean it in an impersonal or notional, catechetical sense. What does it mean to live out the fruits of the Spirit of God in our daily lives? How do we even begin to incorporate these gifts—love, joy, peace, patience, kindness, goodness, faithfulness, gentleness, and self-control—

into our behavior and making that a consistent, daily pattern? This is not a simple process. Precisely, it is what Ignatian spirituality invites us to through a process of attentiveness that leads and enables us to find God in all things.

A Meditation (Galatians 5:22–25)

I would like to propose a meditation on the text of Galatians 5:22–25.

Find a comfortable space and assume a comfortable position. Take a few deep breaths. Allow all your senses to become attuned and attentive to your surroundings and environment....

Read the text slowly. Repeat it. Begin to reflect on these questions:

How are the gifts and the presence of Christ reflected in my life and daily living through love and joy?

How am I showing peace and patience?

Where and how am I showing kindness and goodness and bringing light to the lives of others?

How has God been present to me, and how have I been present to God in my daily living, in the ordinary circumstances of my life?

As a woman, how do I experience God in all things through love? Where is God showing me love? Who shows me this gift?

Through whom do I experience the meaning of love in my family, my work, my community?

Reflecting on my day, how loving have I been to myself? Have I been harsh with myself, or have I been kind? Have I been critical of myself in ways that have left me feeling miserable?

Where is the gentle Spirit of God inviting me to further grow and deepen the awareness of the beauty of God's presence in life?

Why Do You Trouble This Woman?

The importance of this meditation is that it invites and empowers us to attend closely to how the unfolding events of our lives are at the same time revelatory of God's presence and of our spiritual growth and maturity. This is important for women who tend to place the needs of others ahead of their own out of love and care for them, be they family, friends, or coworkers. As we meditate and reflect, we intentionally take time to see and grow from the insights shown to us by the work of the Spirit. The Spirit of God whispers in our ears and shows us the path of wisdom and interior peace. But it takes time and attention to understand how to respond in fulfilling and nourishing ways. It takes time and attentiveness to find and recognize God in all things.

What I have identified and called intentional attentiveness is precisely what Ignatius called the Examen. It is a simple, practical, and effective way of seeking and always recognizing the footprints of God as we journey through the ordinary circumstances of our lives.

Kate had found herself miserable and angry, but by paying attention to the events and moments of her daily living, and especially the uncomfortable ones, she began to see that she needed to speak the truth—first to herself and then to her husband. Instead of piling blame on herself and wallowing in resentment and self-pity, she discovered that she could step back and serenely and clearly see what was really going on. In this way, she found a path of wisdom that led to inner peace. She acknowledged her anger and how it was damaging her relationship with her husband. Not in anger but in a truthful response, Kate found the courage to speak out of her reality. Fortunately, her husband responded with love.

This experience of truth telling is a nugget of wisdom in the *Exercises* that has been overlooked. In the rush to create an inventory or court record of the retreatant's sins and sinfulness, it is easy to forget that the goal is not to reprimand or to apportion blame. For us as women, it is an invitation to formulate, speak, and own our truth no matter the circumstances. Because of the many overlays of painful experiences that many women have encountered in the process of growing up, for some it may take a long period of self-reflection to release the gifts of the Spirit into their lives. At a time when many women are naming their negative experiences, including abuse and exploitation, this process of truth telling can be disconcerting and painful.

Yet, to be open to the fruits and gifts of the Spirit, the woman of the *Exercises* must assume the courage to face the necessary truth telling and reflection to readjust her perspectives and perceive the strength and grace in herself, and thus become empowered to stand on her own two feet and be proud, happy, and at home with herself and with the God of her desires, dreams, and longings.

The *Spiritual Exercises* offers every woman the opportunity to be truthful first with herself. As mentioned, this might mean reflecting on the ways she may have inadvertently or unwittingly participated in her self-denigration, or even abuse, by withdrawing from truth telling, by accepting the definition of others regarding her gifts and capacities, and by creating negative narratives about herself, all of which reinforce and are reinforced by religious beliefs, societal norms, and cultural constructs.

This kind of truth telling is also necessary for the woman who grew up having everything and lacking nothing without any apparent experience of mistreatment or exploitation. For this woman, a different kind of truth telling may be necessary. It may entail recognizing her self-absorption and the tendency to place herself ahead of others. For it may be that this woman has grown up believing that she is living out what is expected of her only to find that when God directs God's loving gaze at her, she too is invited to live more radically the call to a life of grace that sees the needs of others and tends to their fragility and vulnerability.

A FULLY GROWN-UP TREE AND A WALKING STICK

Keeping in mind the theme of finding God in all things, the idea of intentional attentiveness, and the necessity of truth telling as a condition for and manifestation of spiritual growth and maturity, I will explore what happens when women come to the *Spiritual Exercises*. The focus of this exploration is on the spiritual companion. I am drawing on my experience of spiritual companionship over many years as a practitioner of Ignatian spirituality. This exercise is useful for women, as well as for men who are tasked with the role of serving as pointers to the guidance and inspiration of the Spirit (*Spiritual Exercises*, 15). How do we journey with women on their pilgrimage of the *Spiritual Exercises*?

An African proverb says, "A fully grown-up tree cannot be bent into a walking stick." What lesson does this proverb offer us? The primary lesson is the awareness that when women engage with the *Spiritual Exercises*, they come already formed in ways that are deeply, spiritually, and uniquely meaningful to them. In that graced space of spiritual accompaniment, the woman in front of me is already alive with the stirrings, promptings, and inspirations of the Spirit of God. In this space or context, a spiritual companion has the privilege of journeying with her to discover greater depths to her experience of God.

One of my aspirations as a practitioner of Ignatian spirituality and a spiritual companion walking with women in the *Spiritual Exercises* is to provide new wings to the *Exercises* so that the women who come to me and I can fly unhindered and free and soar into new horizons and richness with God. This idea bears further exploration, especially because it could offer deeper insight into the process of accompanying the woman of the *Exercises* for those who are privileged to serve as spiritual companions.

THE WOMAN IN FRONT OF ME

Before embarking on this exploration, let us recall the presence and influence of women on Ignatius and his development of the *Spiritual Exercises* as presented in the previous chapter. In this section is something more practical and pertinent to the entire experience of accompanying women in the *Spiritual Exercises*. From the perspective of a spiritual companion, I would like to imagine the woman who comes for the purpose of engaging with the *Exercises*. Who is she? Who is the woman in front of me? The first thing to pay attention to is her multifaceted reality. She is many things, each of which is space for God's presence to manifest.

The woman of the *Exercises* could have one of several possible backgrounds; she could be a widow, a divorcée, a single woman, a married woman with children or no children. She could be working several jobs. She could be a woman religious with a variety of challenges in her community and ministry. The woman in front of me may be dealing with several personal challenges such as loss, aging, loneliness, and poor health.

The woman of the *Exercises* might be moving along in life with different intensity and resolve, maybe slowly or rapidly. She may even have existential questions about the purpose of her life, the meaning of her commitments, or even the presence or absence of God in her life. Like Kate, she may be keen on prayer, but can find little time and space in the hustle and bustle of her life to sit still and know that God is near.

As Ignatius pointed out in the *Spiritual Exercises*, this woman is coming to "seek and find the divine will" and to "find God in all things." Engaging in the *Spiritual Exercises* is an important step for her in her quest to find who God is for her, what God desires for her, who she is for God, and what she desires of God. The woman in front of me may come with some apprehension and ambiguity about her intentions and the object of her quest, but her desire is pure and noble; she wants to find God and allow God's light and love to squeeze and shine through all the nooks and crannies and cracks of her life.

In this circumstance, what am I as a spiritual companion to do? How should I carry myself in front of the woman of the *Exercises*? From experience, I have found that as a spiritual companion, I am called to wait and to listen deeply. I cannot repeat the importance of this attitude and posture enough. It implies being focused, patient, and attentive to the gentle steps and developments in her walking and wondering and even her running and jumping.

The woman engaged in the *Exercises* is hoping for an adventure of discovery. She desires to unveil her truths and discover her power. She may not realize it, but her reality is the ingredient for God's intervention in and through the *Spiritual Exercises*. She has come with a heart that may be only half-open, but she has stepped through my door. Despite her fear and resistance, she is curious. Where might this adventure lead? She is here to find out how her God is shaping and reshaping her against all odds. Her desire is to align her will with that of her God. My choice of words is deliberate: *her* God, not *my* God.

What does this mean? One of the lessons lies in the proverb "A fully grown-up tree cannot be bent into a walking stick." The woman in front of me and in front of the God of the *Exercises* is a fully grown-up tree that should not be bent—in fact, cannot be bent—into a walking stick. Yet as we saw in previous examples, she may come to the *Exercises* from a society in which she has been considered second class or from a church where her image is often not reflected in her experience of God. She might come from a church where the images of women are sometimes distorted and unrelated to how she sees herself as a woman.

The woman in front of me might be a seeker who has never found a home in any religion or practice. The woman engaged in the adventure of the *Exercises* might never have been given the opportunity to express her deepest desires as a woman. The woman in front of me might have had her authentic voice muted. She might be educated or not educated; she might be of another religion or no religion. She might be well established, strong, and gifted—a woman of many abilities and capabilities.

The woman in front of me might be broken and wondering if anyone can see anything beautiful about her or if she can see anything beautiful about herself. Yet, it is important not to see her as a specimen representative of all women. She might have some shared experiences with other women of what it means to be a woman, but she is one of a kind. She is unique and irreplaceable. Part of my calling as a spiritual companion is to honor her uniqueness.

THE UNIQUENESS OF THE WOMAN IN FRONT OF ME

Let me tell a story that illustrates the uniqueness of the woman who engages in the journey of the *Spiritual Exercises*.

Lola and Tolu are identical twins. Like most identical twins, it was assumed that they would share the same personality and same physical features and would probably be interested in the same things. This could be close to the truth for some identical twins, but not for Lola and Tolu.

Their parents knew early in the twins' lives that they were very different, with unique identities, even though they looked alike. While Tolu was interested in becoming a Catholic nun, Lola was very interested in getting married and looked forward to having children. They were born just a few minutes apart, but they developed very different personalities and interests.

Lola told the story of how she and Tolu realized in first grade that they had different friends. Lola liked the boys and would enjoy being with many people, while Tolu was more interested in telling Bible stories and singing songs and reaching out to people. Tolu was always ready to help anyone. She was sometimes called "Little Mother Teresa." She once said, "I learned from a very young age from my mother, who was always very caring to people. My mom tells us stories of nuns who trained her and were always there to help her and her friends when she was in school. I grew up just wanting to help others." Tolu's personality was that of a reserved person but who was always sensitive and present to others.

Lola was outgoing and enjoyed partying, and she would often be upset that she was left out in family issues. She once complained, "Why am I always the last person to know what's happening in this house?" She was not angry, but surprised that things would have happened, and she was never in the loop.

Nevertheless, in their differences, Lola and Tolu shared much love and laughter. The good thing about the different personalities, interests, and hobbies of these twins was that they were never compared to each other. They grew into their unique personalities. They were never afraid to express themselves.

As mentioned, the point of this story is an invitation to imagine, recognize, and celebrate the uniqueness of every human. This quality is particularly pertinent for the woman who embarks on the journey of the *Spiritual Exercises*. Journeying with her requires respectful attentiveness to her unique paths and deep desires.

Still on this notion of uniqueness, let us consider a scriptural story. In John 4:1–42, we meet the woman at the well, or rather, she meets Jesus at the well. Her interaction with Jesus was unique and personal. The place of meeting was unique, the mode of conversation was unique, and the nature of the encounter was unique.

Although unnamed, she resembles the woman of the *Spiritual Exercises* because she came as her own person. She was the beauty and presence of the God of life. She came not as another, but as uniquely herself with her stories, dreams, and desires. She cut the figure of the woman of the *Exercises* who has always longed to come to God as she was—to express her truest desires to be the person she knows she is called to be— yet she finds it difficult to find and to experience the Divine and to follow her God accordingly.

Like the woman at the well, she is always eager to spread goodness; she wants to go back and bring others to God. She wants to express herself the way she has encountered the Divine, yet she is afraid to do so because society, culture, and religion impose impediments, hindrances, and obstacles in her path.

If you are a spiritual companion reading this, journeying with this kind of woman poses a challenge for the exercise of spiritual companionship: Are you able to be still, silent, large-hearted, and respectful enough to recognize that the woman in front of you is sui generis, like no other?

A GUIDED MEDITATION

Take a moment for a simple exercise that pulls together the key themes and insights of this chapter, especially the truth about the uniqueness of the woman of the *Exercises* and of your own uniqueness.

Find a comfortable space and assume a comfortable position. Take a few deep breaths. Allow all your senses to become attuned and attentive to your surroundings and environment....

Imagine yourself sitting in front of God. Where is God meeting with you? Be yourself, be your truth, be your desire, be you....

Imagine your God sitting with you. Meet your God as you are. Relax and feel the comfort and consolation of God's presence. A presence that is welcoming, renewing, and empowering, just like the encounter between the woman at the well and Jesus.

Why Do You Trouble This Woman?

Recall the beauty and gift of your personality. Slowly and deliberately, as in a colloquy, begin to speak to God about yourself and your journey. Share your heart with your God....

I come here and I sit in front of you.
I come here and I look at you looking at me.
I come here and I see you noticing me.
I come here with a heart full of questions.
I come here with a life full of adventures.
I come here with some apprehension and ambiguity.
I come here not even sure how I got here.
I come here as a seeker, looking for something that is mine.
I come here from a kind of homelessness and a desire to belong.
I come here wanting to find myself again.
I come here because I believe I am meant to be here.
I come here because you want me to be here.
I come here because you know my name and you called me.
I come here because I am unique for you.
I come here... (add whatever thoughts come to your mind from the depths of your heart).

3

Women's Bodies and the God of Our Bodies

The body of a tortoise is also its house.

—An African proverb

In the previous chapter, I explored the pivotal notion in Ignatian spirituality of finding God in all things and how women might more intentionally engage in this practice in their spiritual lives. This connection was premised on the central point I made in the first chapter concerning the integral connection between the development of Ignatius's spiritual consciousness and the role and contribution of women to this development, and consequently the affinity between women and the *Spiritual Exercises*. Women have played and continue to play a significant role in shaping Ignatian spirituality. This role goes all the way back to the infancy of Ignatius; Ignatian spirituality bears the decisive mark and imprint of the feminine genius.

The more I have progressed in my spiritual journey, and in the privileged experience of accompanying others on their journey, the more I have become convinced that this relationship

43

between Ignatian spirituality and women is not only foundational; it is also enduring. It continues to yield insights on how women "draw profit" (to use an Ignatian term) from their exposure to and practice of this spirituality in general.

In this chapter, I explore another theme that relates in a unique way to women's experience and practice of Ignatian spirituality, namely, the importance of an embodied spiritual encounter in prayer and contemplation. This represents another dimension of Ignatian spirituality that is particularly apt for women.

As I mentioned in previous chapters, the woman who embraces the adventure of the *Spiritual Exercises* does so holistically. No part of her life or her experience is off limits. She comes as she is and brings into this graced moment who she is in her entirety. This embodied quality is encouraged in the *Spiritual Exercises*. The exhortation to the retreatant to use all the senses in contemplation is a central feature of the *Exercises*. As a woman, I consider this feature an invitation to pay attention to and connect all my life's dimensions with God's loving presence in my spiritual experience. As a woman, I am called to live out my spiritual encounter in my body entirely, completely, and fully.

In making this point about Ignatian spirituality and embodiment, I am not oblivious to some challenges that confront this reality in the lives of women. To set my reflection on the critical importance of embodiment in context, I would like to consider two key issues, namely, the violence done against women's bodies and the fear of women's bodies.

THE WOUNDS AND FEARS OF A WOMAN'S BODY

As an African woman, I am deeply conscious of the fact that women's bodies are often battered by a myriad of cultural, religious, and societal factors. Think, for example, of the experience of sexual, gender-based violence, or the exclusion of women from leadership roles in the sacramental life of the church. We could also consider several other social privileges that are denied women, including work, ownership of property, inheritance rights, education, and maternal health, exclusively on account of their gender. These denials inflict wounds on women's bodies.

Yet ironically, one of the foundational metaphors for the church is the body of Christ. Properly considered, it is an inclusive and holistic symbolism except, as is often the case, when it comes to women. I recall the message of the 1994 African Synod to the women of Africa. The message was direct, incisive, and uplifting—almost prophetic. In part, the synod declared, "You [Catholic women] are often the back bone of the local Church...a great force for the apostolate of the Church."[1] I have often wondered about the implications of this powerful statement especially as mentioned in an ecclesial context in which women often experience exclusion. If the synod is right, several consequences follow.

First, the multiple forms of violence visited on women in places such as Africa are wounds inflicted on the community called church. Therefore, second, neither theology nor spirituality that is sensitive to the needs of women can circumvent their reality of woundedness. Third, to be holistic and authentic, the narrative of women's spirituality should be capable of accounting for the giftedness and woundedness of women. Ignatian spirituality as represented in the *Spiritual Exercises* is a robust space wherein these two dimensions converge for women to tell their stories as well as recognize, affirm, integrate, and celebrate their giftedness as the *imago Dei*.

Furthermore, this third point is not self-evident. From the discussion in the previous chapter, as women we must discover the space in spirituality for this reality to become true for us, which is partly the purpose of this book.

In a concrete and practical sense, to speak of women's bodies in the context of any tradition of spirituality is to recognize the life-giving quality of those bodies. In this regard, I am reminded of the poignant observation of British theologian Tina Beattie, linking the life-giving quality of women to the sacrifice of Christ: "To give birth is to make a blood sacrifice, a sacrifice of one's own blood. It is to say, 'This is my body, this is my blood, given for you.'"[2] Thus, if spirituality is about affirming life, as I am convinced it is, women practice it with holistic intent and integral commitment, that is, with their whole being. Thus, for a woman, corporeity is not antithetical to spirituality. Women understand this experience; they enrich the spirituality of the body of Christ by it.

However, there is another dimension that links corporeity and spirituality, namely, the fear of women's bodies. One scriptural passage that brings this realization home for me is the story of the woman with a flow of blood (Mark 5:24–43). As an African woman, I have seen firsthand the fixation on the flow of blood and how this fixation distorts the image of women in cultural settings. Such a fixation ignores the fact that women's bleeding is not merely the outcome of a naturally occurring biological phenomenon. What causes women to bleed is more structural than natural. The cause of bleeding for many women is essentially a constellation of evil: poverty; sexual, gender-based violence; and discrimination. Let me make an important note here: Though I have intentionally focused my reflections on women, other groups of people may have experienced similar woundedness and stigma. We need to recognize and honor their pain and stories as well.

Like the women in the gospel narratives, women still have to push through a multiplicity of formidable barriers and obstacles in their determined quest to touch the body of the risen Christ with their own wounded bodies to seek healing and wholeness in ways that only they can experience on account of the integrity of their bodies and spirits. This idea of touch leads to another important point about embodied spirituality as practiced by women.

Don't Touch Me? (John 20:1–18)

Besides the story of the unnamed woman who struggled to touch Jesus, scripture offers us another striking narrative of bodily touch as a constitutive dimension of the spiritual encounter and experience of women. The story of the dawn encounter between Mary Magdalene and the risen Christ at the resurrection is familiar (John 20:1–18). I evoke it not merely to make an exegetical point but to underline why from my perspective as a woman it serves to reinforce the link between spirituality and corporeity. As I imagine this story in the context of contemplative prayer—rather than exegetically—it is a story of an embodied encounter with the risen Jesus that in the final analysis is what spirituality means for me as a woman and by extension what Ignatian spirituality calls us to do in its expression in the *Spiritual Exercises*. Whether in contemplation, through our imagination, or in a colloquy, through our words, we are always engaging the Divine with our entire being—body, soul, mind, and spirit.

I would love to have been a fly on the wall of Jesus's tomb during his postresurrection encounter with Mary Magdalene. We will never know what transpired between the two. Its interpretation or perception is perhaps one of the most contested in Christian tradition. In my imaginative reconstruction, a few things strike me. With due consideration for how various exegetes and experts interpret *"noli mi tangere"*—"don't touch me," "do not hold on to me," "don't cling to me," and so on—it is hard to imagine the risen Christ barking these words as a warning, a rebuke, or a deterrent. Certainly, not to a friend who was even prepared to go and take his body wherever they may have displaced it. It is a safe assumption that Mary Magdalene had no plans to lift the body of her beloved "Rabboni" with a mechanical crane; her desperation at the missing body of Jesus and her determination to find and retrieve it reminds me of Mary cradling the body of her limp and lifeless son in Michelangelo's iconic sculpture, *Pietà*.

As I imagine this scene in contemplative prayer, Mary Magdalene did what every friend would do with a beloved, and especially one who has been unavoidably absent on account of a tragic event. I imagine her reaching out lovingly to embrace the risen Christ. She was fearless and uninhibited by social, cultural, and religious norms that policed such embodied meetings. This post-resurrection encounter of affection rendered her powerful beyond the constraints of taboos, sanctions, and prohibitions. Unlike the other disciples with later apparitions, she did not wait to be invited and only later haltingly approached and hesitantly touched the body of the risen Christ. At that instant, near the empty tomb, Mary Magdalene emerged an apostle with no less a mandate than that of her male colleagues: she "went and announced to the disciples, 'I have seen the Lord'" (v. 18). Imagine the sudden and profound transformation from a sobbing, sorrowful, and confused friend to a strong, bold, and eloquent evangelist.

Spirituality is an empowering phenomenon for corporeity if the vital connection is properly understood, recognized, and appropriately celebrated. That is part of what Mary Magdalene teaches us and what women bring to the traditions of spirituality such as Ignatian spirituality. This is how spirituality becomes holistic, inclusive, and mystical.

Approaching this story as an African woman who is familiar with the narratives of many African women forced to labor under silencing and enslaving cultural, societal, and religious impositions, I find an even more potent, liberating dimension to the Johannine narrative. Mary Magdalene broke a taboo not in the legalistic sense of violating an injunction, but in the active, defiant, and resistant sense where she declared an end to a yoke and a burden that had hung for centuries on end over countless women, myself included. She dared to touch the body of the risen Christ with the same body that had been violated, ridiculed, and reviled as promiscuous and evil by an oppressive, patriarchal hermeneutics founded on a false construction of what it means to be human. She demonstrated that even our woundedness is a channel of graced and gifted encounters with the source of life.

Like the Lucan woman with a flow of blood, this disciple, Mary Magdalene, broke a taboo. Unlike the former, who did it with trembling and trepidation, Mary Magdalene did so under the empowering glare of the glory of the risen Christ in response to a loving and compassionate call by the one who knew her by name. This is an image of a spiritually liberating moment that I as an African woman and many of my sisters can comprehend, own, and recreate over and over in the sacred space of reflection, meditation, and contemplation. In this space, we declare that we have touched the risen Christ with all our woundedness and giftedness, and we testify that the risen Christ has touched us with the healing, empowering, and transforming presence of God. This in sum is what spirituality means from an embodied perspective. It was not possible for Mary Magdalene to touch and be touched by the risen Christ without going forth to preach and proclaim the good news.

I should mention here that this reality was not lost on Pope Francis when he made the bold move of elevating the simple memorial of Mary Magdalene (July 22) to the status of Feast in the eucharistic celebration of her life and significance in the Christian tradition. Affirming centuries of theological tradition, Francis recognized Mary Magdalene as the *apostolorum apostola*, apostle of the apostles, and a true and authentic evangelizer

Why Do You Trouble This Woman?

in the context of reflecting "in a more profound way on the dignity of Woman."[3] Francis's praise for her knows no bounds:

> This woman, known as the one who loved Christ and who was greatly loved by Christ, and was called a "witness of Divine Mercy" by Saint Gregory the Great and an "apostle of the apostles" by Saint Thomas Aquinas, can now rightly be taken by the faithful as a model of women's role in the Church.[4]

But sadly, old habits die hard. Mary Magdalene's story remains unfinished. In this regard, I am baffled by two facts. The preface composed for the Feast of Mary Magdalene is appropriately captioned "Preface of the Apostle of the Apostles." It contains a narrative reconstruction of the post-resurrection encounter between her and Jesus:

> He appeared in the garden
> and revealed himself to Mary Magdalene,
> who had loved him in life,
> witnessed him dying on the Cross,
> sought him as he lay in the tomb,
> and was the first to adore him, newly risen from the
>   dead.
> He honored her with the office of being an apostle
>   to the Apostles,
> so that the good news of new life
> might reach the ends of the earth.[5]

Largely accurate and positive, this reconstruction leaves out one crucial detail of Mary Magdalene's vital, life-affirming experience: prior to adoring him, she reached out to touch his risen body. To put it differently, her manner of adoration was not the customary detached and disembodied practice; hers was tactile and embodied in flesh and in spirit. As noted above, as a woman and in the context of spirituality, this is not an insignificant detail. Eliding this tactile intimacy between Mary Magdalene and the risen Christ has consequences: left unchallenged, it reinforces centuries of gender-based hermeneutical and exegetical biases that exacerbate the condition of women in church and society by undermining our humanity, sanctity, and sexuality. In fact, one of the inescapable paradoxes of Christianity is the contrast between negative views on the (im)morality of tactility and the centrality of the incarnation. Also, notice how this Johannine scene contrasts with Ignatius's imaginative idea in the *Exercises* (*Spiritual Exercises*, 219) that the risen Christ appeared to his blessed Mother first before anybody else. Was Ignatius a victim of mediaeval attempts to dethrone Mary Magdalene, presumably a woman of tainted reputation, as the first to whom the risen Christ appeared, even possibly touching the resurrected Lord?

The second fact is that the prayer composed by Pope Francis for the Year of Mercy seemingly replicates some atavistic stereotypes, caricatures, and unflattering nomenclature:

> Your loving gaze freed Zacchaeus and Matthew from being enslaved by money; the adulteress and Magdalene from seeking happiness only in created things; made Peter weep after his betrayal, and assured paradise to the repentant thief.[6]

In so writing, the pope aligned himself with other contemporary voices steeped in an erroneous, biased, and unjust portrayal of Mary Magdalene such as in a six-part documentary produced by the Smithsonian Institute in 2008. In the segment of the first episode, "Flesh and Blood," of the documentary, *Decoding Christianity*, the narrator, Christy Kenneally, glibly named Mary Magdalene as "an adulteress."[7] Indeed, the distortion of Mary

Magdalene's story continues, as do the troubles of her sisters in church and society. Yet she refuses to be silent or silenced. From the perspective of this book, her story is a powerful illustration and validation of women's embodied approach to and practice of spirituality.

Hence, to understand the audacity of Mary Magdalene's touch and the injunction of the risen Christ, "Do not cling to me," it would be permissible to eliminate any suggestion of contradiction between the former's bodily gesture and the latter's verbal injunction. There is an important connection between both, but it is not negative.

At first sight, the encounter appears to hinge and perhaps even founder on a seemingly strong prohibition: "Jesus said to her: *noli me tangere*." Yet in the context of contemplative imagination and recalling the point that I made above, upon deeper consideration, rather than repulse her, Jesus's words evoked and affirmed the intimate tactility of the encounter. Mary Magdalene experienced a profound relationship in her touching and seeing the risen Christ in a way none of the male disciples could ever have imagined possible or have experienced. Precisely because Mary Magdalene touched the risen Christ, she was empowered by Christ to announce the resurrection with credibility and authenticity as a friend, a witness, a disciple, and an apostle. As did Paul and the other apostles, she too could proclaim, "What was from the beginning, what we have heard, what we have seen with our eyes, what we looked at and touched with our hands,... we have seen it and testify to it,...we declare to you what we have seen and heard so that you also may have fellowship with us" (1 John 1:1–3).

I have engaged in this extended excursus on women's bodies—the unjustified fears and the unjust wounds associated with them and Mary Magdalene's audacious and loving touch of the body of the risen Christ—to reinforce the fundamental conviction that corporeity is an asset to spirituality and especially Ignatian spirituality.

To pursue the central idea in this section a little further, we might recall how for centuries philosophers and theologians have debated the meaning, importance, and place of the sense of touch. Despite a long tradition of the moralization of touch, which suggests that it is the root of sexual failings, advances in modern science, in particular neuroscience, show the delicate and sophisticated mechanism of touch and its vital importance to human development and survival. How, for example, might we express emotions and affections in casual and intimate relationships without the sense of touch—holding hands, embracing, patting, comforting, and hugging one another? Nor must we ignore the dark side of touch or the perversion of tactility, so evident in recent times in shocking revelations of clergy sexual abuse of minors and sexual harassment of vulnerable people in all domains of social interaction.

The critical point of all this is that as a woman, I express my spirituality as an embodied experience. No part of my life or experience is excluded. Like the tortoise, whose body is also its house, I come as I am and bring who I am in the totality of my being into this graced moment. Like other women whose narratives we heard in the previous chapter, I embody in my life and work the presence and gifts of the Spirit; I am at home with divinity in my body.

I am convinced that women embody and practice Ignatian spirituality with the burden and grace of their lived reality. Yet ours is not an esoteric experiment with spirituality; spirituality connects strongly all the desires, longings, movements, stories, and flows that reveal the presence of divinity in the totality of our lives.

EMBODIMENT AND SPIRITUALITY

Having set the theological and biblical context quite extensively above, albeit from the perspective of a contemplative imagination, I apply this idea of embodiment more practically to the experience of women. I am keen on stressing how such an approach can be a gift to spirituality, in general, not just by women and for women but for all those who seek a space to reconcile their woundedness and their giftedness and to live the ensuing grace with confidence and joy. For this exercise, I invite readers to reflect on their perceptions and experiences of embodiment as they relate to their understanding and practice of spirituality. Let's do a quick reflection:

> Pause for a moment and reflect. When you hear or think of the word *embodiment*, what immediately comes to mind? As a woman (or as a man, as appropriate), what does it recall to your mind? Do you think of your giftedness, uniqueness, capacities, genius? Or does it stir up a mix of fear, frustration, woundedness? Stay with your feelings for a while....

I invite you to pay attention to all the bodily and physical experiences that are unique to us as women from childhood to adulthood and much later in life including, for example, our awesome and transformative experience that heralds our capacity to birth new life, sexual relationships that sometimes could be problematic, or even the experience of menopause. Again, when you think of embodiment, do you recall your giftedness or simply an irritating cyclical or hormone-induced change?

The intended lesson here is that, as women, when we embark on the adventure of the *Spiritual Exercises*, if we are attentive and present to the totality of our experiences as we ought to be, we have neither the excuse nor the option of ignoring our bodily and feminine realities. Our physical body colors and illumines our spiritual paths because, for women, spirituality unfolds along the axis of the body and self. Neither the unnamed woman with a flow of blood nor Mary Magdalene would have known Jesus more intimately, loved Jesus more intensely, and followed Jesus more closely without coming close enough to touch Jesus with their bodies (*Spiritual Exercises*, 104). When Ignatius invites the retreatant to this intimate knowledge of Jesus in the *Spiritual Exercises*, he is not counseling an out-of-body experience. Quite the contrary. He is inviting us to a knowledge of Jesus as he is for us and as we are for him.

The person who says this best is feminist theologian Elizabeth Johnson. Like Tina Beattie, she wrote about the connections of our physical selves as women and how we mirrored creation profoundly in the cycle of life. We are gifts of nature herself, and we are closely interrelated to the seasons of life. Her words deserve to be quoted:

> Hence the world is holy, nature is holy, bodies are holy, women's bodies are holy. For the Spirit creates what is physical—worlds, bodies, senses, sexuality, passions—and moves in these every bit as much as in minds and ideas. About the Creator Spirit this can be said: loves bodies, loves to dance. The whole complex, material universe is pervaded and signed by her graceful vigor.[8]

Considering Johnson's powerful statement, think of the lyrics of Psalm 139:14: "I am fearfully and wonderfully made." As a woman, this is a license to move my body, to rouse my spirit, and to dance to the graceful vigor of the creator Spirit.

Thus, for the woman of the *Exercises*, a heartfelt knowledge of God is not simply disembodied and disincarnate. Nor is it merely intellectual or general. It is experiential, an intentional act of love. I can know God and be known by God only if I come close to God and allow God to draw near to me in the totality of my being—close enough to touch one another. We know our bodies contain deep mysteries. Think of Mary of Nazareth keeping, pondering, and treasuring the deep mysteries of God's ways in her heart (Luke 2:19). We come to encounter and know God through the gift of embodiment. The woman who enters the exhilarating pilgrimage of the *Spiritual Exercises* comes with her entire history embedded in her body and self. She has stories to tell through the pathways of her body's experiences, and she brings that journey with her as she engages with the God of her life. Her story is not just a compilation of words; her story is her life told through the giftedness, woundedness, and concreteness of her body.

In Africa, there is a saying, "A person is a person through other persons." This saying is quite popular and familiar. In fact, it is shorthand for the cultural philosophical concept of *ubuntu*, which is further synthesized in the pithy saying "I am because we are." I am convinced that women incarnate this saying because they are intensely relational. The journey through the *Spiritual Exercises* invites and allows us to bring and unpack the bundle of relationships that integrate our whole being—body, soul, and spirit—graced by the loving gaze of the Divine.

Sadly, women's bodies, feelings, emotions, and desires have been caged, judged, and condemned for a long time, using scripture, culture, religion, and tradition. Sometimes, it makes me wonder what became of the biblical truth that our bodies were temples of the living God or the mystical revelation that every woman is fashioned in the image and likeness of God. These are deep truths about women's identities and bodies that do not exist apart from women's spiritualities. Our deepest truths and moments of encounter with the Divine are rooted in body and self. This ought to be a cause for celebration, not for caution, as our social, cultural, and religious contexts often attempt to foist on us.

The key lesson from the foregoing is that the combination of my body and self is a sacred space for an encounter with the Divine. Women's bodies are sacramental. No truth could be simpler and clearer than that. The question then becomes, How do we translate this embodied truth or truth of embodiment into our experience of the *Spiritual Exercises* as retreatants or spiritual companions or both? This question is an invitation to women to discover, relish, and enjoy their awareness of how God is present and active in their bodies and feelings and expressions of who they are.

EMBODIMENT ILLUSTRATED

As women, how can we experience the sacramentality of our bodies and selves as the sacred space of encounter with and revelation of the Divine? Rather than give an abstract answer, I invite you to a simple exercise of discovery. For this exercise, you will need to use all your senses in the same way that the *Spiritual Exercises* invites retreatants to do. This is a practical illustration of what an embodied spirituality feels like.

Take a moment to pause. Find a comfortable place and posture. Take a few deep breaths. Align and attune all your senses to your surroundings and environment. Now reflect in silence....

Imagine yourself as a painter. How would you paint your story in such a way that you could actually smell the paint, feel the brush in your hand, see the colors of your desires, and channel them all into your prayer?

What if you were more musically inclined? A singer or a composer? How would you compose and sing your story in prayer in such a way that you could feel your soul coming alive through your composition, express yourself in the texts, music, and songs of praise and lament, joy and sorrow, delight and disappointment, however the Spirit moves and inspires you?

Or imagine yourself as a dancer. What is to stop you from dancing (in) your prayer to express your feelings of freedom to be who your God wants you to be?

Imagine yourself as someone who is passionate about knitting. Why wouldn't you be welcome to weave and knit your prayer in a way that you could begin to see the colors, patterns, and the style as all God's unfolding love in your life?

Imagine yourself as a designer, an architect, a builder. What's to stop you from constructing and designing your story in your prayer in such a way that you could feel the styles, shapes, materials, and patterns as manifestations of the infinite reality of God in creation and in your life?

Imagine yourself as a chef or a baker. Why not create a recipe of your contemplation and in that recipe begin to see, taste, and smell the texture, aroma, and fragrance of divine love and goodness wafting through the universe of your culinary experience?

You can continue this exercise for as long as you wish by introducing other skills, experiences, and expertise. The possibilities are limitless. The point is that in the spirit of Ignatian spirituality, there is no prayer without our bodies; embodiment is the locus of prayer. This is also what it means to find God in all things as I mentioned in the previous chapter. In the next chapter, I will expand this theme of embodiment by linking it with the importance of the imagination in Ignatian spirituality.

From my perspective as a woman, I believe that one of the best kept secrets of the *Spiritual Exercises* is that it invites and empowers us to encounter the divine using all the gifts and graces God has given us, and that includes using everything in us and what makes us women. This truth is particularly liberating, renewing, and transforming because it implies that we no longer need to accept the negative images or portrayals of our bodies that culture, society, or religion has prefabricated for us; we need only to take the lid off our deepest beings and let goodness flow from within our hearts and souls in prayer and praise of who we are in, with, and for God.

EMBODIMENT AS SPIRITUAL FRIENDSHIP

In continuation of the theme of embodiment and its constitutive place in Ignatian spirituality, let us explore further the gift of embodiment as a path to friendship with the Divine by considering Ignatius's own experience.

In chapter 1, we "heard" a firsthand account by Ignatius of the time when he was recuperating after his painful injury. His feelings were very much part of that moment. In fact, his feelings revealed the direction of his life because it was through the inner movements of his heart that he came to discover the meaning of consolation and desolation and the dynamics of discernment. What I find interesting is that Ignatius did not notice his feelings by thinking about or trying to intellectualize his experience; it was something much more embodied. He experienced a surge of feelings when he gazed at the stars. His heart swelled with emotions when he read about the heroic deeds of the saints. His desires expanded when he imagined the great exploits that lay ahead of him. It was endless. His feelings and emotions were so central to his spiritual experience. When we understand this, we discover an important key for unlocking the graces of the *Spiritual Exercises.*

As did Ignatius, the woman who embarks on the adventure of the *Exercises* has feelings. And like Ignatius, many things can move her to praise her God with her feelings, senses, and emotions. It could be nature; it could be some of the things that I mentioned above such as music, dance, baking, and so on. In each moment, she can use her sensory capacity to enter a sacred space of intimacy with her God. I believe that without touching her feelings, the woman of the *Exercises* will never touch the depths of who God is for her. Also, from the perspective of a spiritual companion, it is important to pay attention to how she feels about using her feelings. Is she afraid perhaps that what she feels isn't good enough? Is she doubting that others will acknowledge her feelings or accept her emotions? How does she feel about living out her embodied spiritual reality?

The *imago Dei* for the woman of the *Exercises* is expressed in her body, spirit, heart, and soul. Her relationship with self and others is a friendship that allows her to be vulnerable in tasting, seeing, touching, hearing, and smelling the reality and the truths of her life no matter how beautiful or ugly, or how joyful or sad it might be.

Ultimately, in the context of Ignatian spirituality, embodiment is another name for friendship. How else can we enter a relationship of friendship without drawing deeply on the well of our feelings and emotions? That is the story and lesson of several women in the scriptures, as I have pointed out and will further demonstrate below. It is also the story of the woman of the *Exercises.* The *Spiritual Exercises* is a path of deep friendship for women—friendship with themselves, friendship with Jesus, and friendship with the Divine.

I have alluded to the grace of the Second Week of the *Spiritual Exercises*: "Ask for an interior knowledge of Jesus, who became human for me, that I may love him more intensely and follow him more closely" (*Spiritual Exercises*, 104). As mentioned, Ignatius is not asking the retreatant to indulge in some intellectual Christological exercise. Not at all. In fact, it is something more anthropological, something more rooted, earthy, incarnate, and embodied because, immediately after saying that, Ignatius asks the retreatant to deploy all the senses and make a composition of place.

For the woman engaged in the adventure of the *Exercises*, embodiment is an invitation to enter a luscious friendship with her God. At the heart of this friendship, she will come to know the God who is ever present in her body of senses and emotions. In this experience, her heart will begin to beat to the rhythm of the heart of the Divine. She will come to hear the words that she is no longer a slave but a daughter and a beloved of a God who is revealing all things to her in love and friendship. She will come to an interior knowledge of her God who is present to her and revealing Godself to her in this unique relationship. Like the story of Kate and Meg in the preceding chapter, her story, her feelings, and her emotions are not the same for every woman; her embodied spirituality is unique and without parallel.

However, if the woman of the *Exercises* has come from the experience of not being free to express feelings and emotions, or if she has been stereotyped as overly emotional and her feelings and emotions considered unimportant or irrelevant, she probably would struggle with praying and listening and responding to God's desire to encounter her in her body, spirit, heart, and soul. And she may not realize that in her adventure of the *Spiritual Exercises*, her body is a repository of her feelings that are genuine paths and avenues of God's revelation in her life and of God's friendship with her.

Those who are privileged to accompany the woman of the *Exercises* need to be sufficiently grounded in their own feelings and emotions to welcome the expressions of her feelings and emotions. They would need to be free enough to refrain from censoring the ways in which she manifests who she is before her God. They should strive to avoid falling into the temptation of the prophet Eli, who judged Hannah as a drunk, but instead ask for grace not only to read her lips but also to hear the cry of her heart, the movements of her body, and the lament of her soul (1 Sam 1:9–28 ERV). It is worth recalling Hannah's retort in the context of the purposes of this book: "Sir, I have not drunk any wine or beer. I am deeply troubled, and I was telling the LORD about all my problems. Don't think I am a bad woman. I have been praying so long because I have so many troubles and am very sad." It should remind us of Jesus's query, "Why do you trouble this woman?"

Thus, in accompanying the woman of the *Exercises*, the graces of attention, sensitivity, and reverence are indispensable to avoid causing her further troubles. These graces enable us not to censor her but to create a safe space for her to express her feelings and encounter the gentle ways that God is being revealed in and through her body and self.

EMBODIMENT AND THE *SPIRITUAL EXERCISES*

Thus far, I have explored the idea that the *Spiritual Exercises* offers us the locus par excellence to connect embodiment and spirituality. We come home to ourselves in the *Spiritual Exercises*. To conclude this part of the reflection on embodiment as a gift of women's spirituality, I will identify the key elements of the *Spiritual Exercises* that demonstrate and emphasize the importance of cherishing our bodies as spaces of contemplative prayer and sacred encounter.

Adopt a posture that works for you

Ignatius mentions that you can kneel, prostrate yourself on the floor, lie face upward, be seated, or stand. The important thing is to find a bodily posture that works for you and to rest there until you are fully satisfied without any anxiety to move on (*Spiritual Exercises*, 76). The key lesson here is that our prayer needs our bodies; the bodily postures we adopt can make a difference in how well we pray.

Composition of Place

Ignatius always asks the retreatant to do a composition of place. How do you make a composition of place? In fact, it is simple: you do it by "imagining the place" and making it as real as possible in all its details (*Spiritual Exercises*, 47). In other words, says Ignatius, you see the place "with the eyes of the imagination", that is, you imagine and recreate the scene of the meditation and contemplation (*Spiritual Exercises*, 91). This invitation to be imaginative could be the key that Ignatian spirituality offers the woman of the *Exercises* to allow her to enter prayer with her whole being—body, spirit, heart, and soul.

Application of the Senses

When we are engaged in contemplation, Ignatius invites us to "use the imagination and apply all five senses" (*Spiritual Exercises*, 121). We do this not to create a fantasy. Far from it. According to Ignatius, it is because we can draw more fruit or profit from our prayer when we enter it with all our sensory capacities.

Colloquy

At the end of our prayer, Ignatius invites us to speak to God in the way one friend speaks to another. Think of Martha and Mary speaking to their friend, Jesus, in Bethany!

A GUIDED MEDITATION

In the preceding section, I identified four elements that are pivotal in the understanding of Ignatian spirituality, as laid out in the *Spiritual Exercises* as an embodied experience. As I understand it, one of the greatest gifts of Ignatian spirituality to the woman of the *Exercises* is the invitation to enter prayer with the giftedness, mystery, and sacredness of her body. She is created to praise, reverence, and serve God, and none of this makes sense without her immersing herself in the encounter with the Divine by involving all her feelings, imagination, intellect, and emotions.

Thus, the *Spiritual Exercises* is an embodied path of prayer; we see this in so many aspects of the *Exercises*, such as composition of place, application of the senses, the posture of prayer, and the colloquy. Furthermore, the gift of embodiment opens a path to spiritual friendship that is unique because the feelings and emotions of the woman of the *Exercises* constitute an unrepeatable gift of relationship with the Divine.

Keeping these points in mind, I invite you to meditate on the story of the woman with the alabaster jar in Luke 7:37–50 (see also Matt 26:6–13; Mark 13:3–9). This reflection is one example among many in the Gospels that foregrounds the reality of embodiment as a path toward friendship with the Divine. Like the woman of the *Exercises*, the woman with the alabaster jar is the woman who Jesus encountered at Simon the Leper's house; she is the woman in front of Jesus. But she is no ordinary woman. Despite the negative judgments of the onlookers, she is not afraid to be in the presence of Jesus, expressing her deep love embodied in her gestures.

As usual, find a conducive space and adopt a comfortable posture. Take a few deep breaths. Align and attune all your senses to your surroundings and environment.

Read verse 38 from this story: "She stood behind him at his feet, weeping, and began to bathe his feet with her tears and to dry them with her hair. Then she continued kissing his feet and anointing them with the ointment." Repeat this verse until the words permeate your senses and stimulate your imagination.

Now pause, take a deep breath, and imagine this woman in front of Jesus. It is an amazing and striking picture. Consider how the four elements highlighted above about embodiment in the *Exercises* apply to her. First, she settles into a comfortable position "behind Jesus, at his feet." Second, she composes the place, not in her imagination but with her entire body. Third, she engages with Jesus using all her senses, her feelings, her body—touch and smell, tears and kisses, fragrance, and hair. Fourth, she bonds with Jesus in a silent heart-to-heart conversation. Imagine the emotional sumptuousness of this scene. It is suffused with the senses, feelings, and emotions.

Now pause again, take a deep breath, and pay attention to what is going on between Jesus and this woman in front of him. Notice how rich her story is. It is not just about wiping Jesus's feet; it is more about her deep love for and her awareness of who Jesus is. She must have known of him and known exactly how to relate with him because Jesus understands the language of her heart embodied in her gestures.

See how Jesus doesn't dismiss her; he welcomes her. Jesus doesn't condemn her; he affirms her. Jesus doesn't scorn her; he accepts her gift of extravagant, overflowing love, embodied in her alabaster jar and poured out lavishly on him.

Again, pause, take a deep breath, and in your imagination notice how this encounter transforms the woman's life. Imagine how she now sees her life, journey, struggles, and giftedness in a new light and feels accepted by God. In your imagination, listen to Jesus saying to the onlookers, "Why do you trouble this woman? This woman has shown me great love."

Now gradually return to yourself. What lesson, fruit, or profit do you draw from this moment? What new spaces does this meditation open for you to encounter the liberating love of

God through your feelings, emotions, and desires? Allow yourself to overcome any intimidation or shyness and see, feel, taste, and notice the presence of the Divine in your life.

Now engage in a conversation with the Divine and ask for the grace to trust your feelings, as did the woman in front of Jesus, to encounter the Divine with freedom and to know yourself as loved and known as you are and empowered to celebrate the gift of friendship, the ability of being vulnerable in the presence of another, and the ability to pray with your body in the overflowing, extravagant fragrance of your soul as an avenue of divine love.

As you continue this moment of graced encounter, imagine the Divine sitting with you. Feel the Divine holding you and watching you praise and reverence the Divine with all that you are. Conclude your meditation with these words:

> Love of my life, my body, and my soul, you created
>   me to be fully alive.
> You created me to share life, love, and laughter in
>   my being.
> You called me to be in relationship with you as you
>   draw close to me, that I may have life and have it
>   in full.
> I come home to myself in you, my love.
> You make me feel authentic in the totality of my
>   being as a woman in front of you.
> My heart overflows with your love.

4

The Gift and the God of Imagination

The cricket says it can sing and dance elegantly, but the chicken prevents it from displaying its skills in broad daylight.

—An African proverb

In the previous chapter, we explored the idea, practice, and experience of embodiment as an integral and constitutive dimension of women's practice of spirituality. I made the point that such practice is particularly suited to and encouraged by Ignatian spirituality in its expression in the *Spiritual Exercises*. This idea was anchored in chapter 2, in which I gave examples of what it means to find God in all things and especially what that means for women through their daily and lived experiences.

As noted, these approaches are founded in my primary thesis, or rather my conviction of the mutuality between Ignatian spirituality and women's practice of spirituality. More importantly, the formation of Ignatius's spiritual consciousness, his spiritual development, and his spiritual legacy owe much to the influence and contribution of women—the thread that runs through this book.

In this chapter, we further extend and expand the reflection by considering another unique aspect of Ignatian spirituality in its expression in the *Spiritual Exercises*: the gift of imagination. As usual, this is not a general examination. The focus and intent remain on women and how their multiple experiences create new paths that draw on the resources of Ignatian spirituality. How does the gift of imagination open a pathway into Ignatian spirituality for women?

THE HIDDEN GOD

As already noted, Ignatius has several insights in the *Spiritual Exercises*. They are like nuggets of wisdom, unrefined and shocking at times but profoundly fascinating and illuminating when we take time to consider them or as Ignatius would say "mull them over from time to time" (*Spiritual Exercises*, 164). Here is one example:

> When I made the *Spiritual Exercises* in its thirty-day format, I was quite shocked to come across this statement: "Consider how his [Jesus's] divinity hides itself" (*Spiritual Exercises*, 196). This occurs in the Third Week of the *Exercises* in the context of Jesus's passion and suffering. Ignatius then suggests that the suffering Jesus appears to be a pale image of the powerful and transcendent God who "could destroy his enemies but does not, and…allows his most holy humanity to suffer so cruelly."
>
> Ignatius's words align with a similar insight of Gustavo Gutierrez, which I read several years ago. Gutierrez talked about a hidden God: "The Lord hides his presence in history, and at the same time

reveals it, in the life and suffering, and struggles, the death, and the hopes of the condemned of the earth."[1]

In one sense, this idea of hiddenness of divinity could focus the mind of the retreatant on the aspect of loss. The resulting disposition could be despair and despondence. If divinity is absent, hidden, or hiding, where can one find light or hope to continue? Here again is one interesting aspect of the genius of Ignatius and Ignatian spirituality in general. What you see is not always what you get.

In the larger context of the Third Week of the *Spiritual Exercises*, to say that divinity is hidden does not amount to a call to despair; rather, it is an invitation to faith. The retreatant is invited to continue to see God's presence amid Jesus's darkness, pain, and suffering. How is this vision of God in a space of darkness possible? A powerful and effective tool for this is the gift of the imagination.

The use of the imagination in the *Spiritual Exercises* is key. There are several variants of its use. In the previous chapter, we saw the exercise of composition of place. For every exercise of meditation or contemplation, we are invited to recreate the scene. The unique feature of Ignatian composition of place is that the retreatant does not stand outside this place; she or he is in it. For this reason, she or he is invited to apply all the five senses to bring the scene of contemplation to life and to situate herself or himself in it.

In the nativity scene, for example, Ignatius invites the retreatant to take an actual and concrete role, in this case that of a servant: "I will make myself a poor, little, and unworthy slave, gazing at them, contemplating them, and serving them in their needs, *just as if I were there*, with all possible respect and reverence" (*Spiritual Exercises*, 114; emphasis mine). The use of the imagination in Ignatian spirituality is anything but a transposition into the status of a bystander or spectator. Contemplative imagination draws us into the heart of prayer and enables us to experience the presence of God in the contemplative moment as if we were there.

Imagination enriches prayer, reflection, meditation, and contemplation. There is always the danger of confusing it with fantasy. In Ignatian spirituality, imagining does not simply run wild; imagining creates a space of encounter where it becomes possible to meet God even in God's seeming absence and to trust in God's presence in the moment of contemplative prayer.

THE GIFT OF IMAGINATION IN THE STORIES OF AFRICAN WOMEN

To explore the gift of the imagination and its pivotal importance for women engaging in the *Exercises*, I offer a narrative of my experience of spirituality in an African context and apply some of its insight to a deeper understanding of Ignatian spirituality. By doing this, I intend to reinforce the idea that the imagination is a special gift to women when it comes to walking the path of Ignatian spirituality.

Over the years, I have been amazed by the capacity of African women to imagine God in ways that are diametrically different from received wisdom and Western approaches. I believe that this capacity demonstrated by African women is a gift to theology and spirituality. Obviously, there is a way in which imagination is limited. No matter how versatile, this power of the mind can never fully encompass the mystery of God. Divinity always overflows the limits of our comprehension and imagination even to the point of hiding itself. There is always a sense of something greater than us, a mystery beyond our understanding that is profoundly disconcerting and deeply comforting at the same time. But because of the power of the imagination, we are also aware of the intimacy of mystery.

What I find particularly refreshing is that it is in exercising the gift of my imagination as a woman that I can break the mold of patriarchy, androcentrism, and sexism that produces only one limited and alienating image of God. Thus, the fixation on the maleness of God crumbles before the power of my imagination to see the God in whose image and likeness I was fashioned. This is something that happens almost routinely in my prayer.

As we have seen so far, the lives and stories of women such as Mary Magdalene and her sisters in scripture demonstrate the power of women to imagine another God possible, a God who does not hold women captive to masculine power and domination and the attendant prejudice, stereotyping, and discrimination based on their gender. Rather, in the lives of these women, we are able to imagine God's liberating tenderness and love.

From my experience with accompanying many women as a spiritual companion, I have come to realize that as women, the gift of our imagination reveals a profound disposition and orientation toward loving, compassionate, and life-giving endeavors. This disposition is not merely reducible to a maternal desire in its gendered form; it is a much deeper reality. When God reveals Godself as love, a life giver, and a healer, this is a mystery I can imagine in my own being as a woman. This is a revelation that I can translate through my imagination and my prayer as a call to love, to give life, and to include, heal, and affirm. From this perspective, imagination does not dissolve into fantasy; imagination always calls to action and generates a profound desire to engender a new ethos of life and care for the other that is rooted in relationality.

As mentioned above, when it comes to breaking the mold and hold of patriarchy, imagination is a key asset. From experience, I know that many African women express their understanding of God as masculine and feminine, even though the main religions in Africa speak of God in masculine terminology.

In their imagination, the mystery of God transcends the predominant maleness of God. Using their imagination, they are perfectly capable of relativizing and neutralizing the hold of this maleness. In the religious worldview and spiritual imagination of an African woman, God is everything: "In God, we live and move and have our being" (see Acts 17:28).

The creativity of African women's imagination of who God is is often reflected in the names that describe their experiences of daily life. African women have many descriptive names and images of the one God—as many as her daily personal experiences—that encompass a myriad of God's actions, being, and encounters with human beings. Accordingly, the African woman sees and imagines God as the sole creator of the universe, and her experience of giving life mirrors the attribute of God as giver of life. The African woman knows from experience that God creates and holds the world together and that no single word or symbol exhausts the concept of God. This allows her to deploy her imagination extensively and creatively without limiting God to one set of descriptors that impoverish the mystery of God.

For an African woman, God simply means life such that she can personify her every experience in the light of God's image. As I mentioned above, this imaginative giftedness allows her to relativize gender as the organizing principle of mystery and transcendence. Thanks to the gift of her imagination, the African woman effortlessly perceives God not as male or female albeit African women will speak of God as Father. The African woman speaks in a language that is purely religious and spiritual. If a Westerner would engage an African woman in a conversation of any sort, she would make constant reference to God as "the all in all, present in all things," and she might use the masculine pronoun he or perhaps refer to God as she. In most African languages, there are no gender-specific terms;

she is not wedded to one dogmatic nomenclature or linguistic framework.

Thus, beyond what is theologically or even dogmatically defined as normative, what is important for the African woman is to know God. She has an interior experience of the Divine that is almost palpable. Her experiences constitute her primary revelatory texts. It is not a theory that she learns from a book. She finds joy in singing and praying to her father and mother God who has blessed her with life. Her image of God is as boundless as the presence of the Divine in all creation is infinite. The African woman's encounter with God is reflected in her God who is the light on her path when she is not sure of her journey, the provider who surprises her with some food for her family through the kindness of a neighbor, the protector who rescues her from the violence she often encounters in society. All these profoundly rich experiences speak to the power and the gift of imagination.

In a very real sense, these names are expressions of who God is for the African woman—everything. In fact, the words themselves will have little or no meaning if she does not touch the underlying reality and the underlying experience of who God is as expressed in the names she uses for God.

The expression of God for an African woman is not set aside for a particular occasional experience called worship or liturgy. Rather, it is like the air she breathes. There is no experience outside of God. Her religious language is her breath and her body, soul, and spirit. The Divine is present in all creation and experiences including birthing, dying, eating, sleeping, dancing, loving, protecting, and so on. Here again we see the idea that I have repeated in previous chapters that no part of the story of the woman of the *Exercises* is off limits.

In these names for God, we hear echoes of the experiences of African women. In their experience of God, these African women understand the limitations of concepts and words to comprehend the Divine. But using the power and gift of their imagination, a whole new space of understanding and encounter begins to emerge. When African women pile up rocks around a fire to support a pot to cook a meal for their families, spread themselves out to shelter and protect their families, nurse their children to life, sing of the great spirits, set the hoe to earth to grow food for their communities, trek for miles to draw water to feed and clean their children...ineffability coincides with spirituality and their stories and experiences reveal and celebrate a divinity that defies mere rhetoric, repels the profane gaze of patriarchal scrutiny, and evades the dungeons of metaphysical categories. In other words, God becomes incarnate in the stories of African women.

It is no surprise, therefore, that African women theologians often imagine Christ as one who opens doors to freedom, as one who delivers the people from the woes and miseries of starvation and provides cleansing water. This is a Christ who leads us to human ways of living. The African Christian woman knows a God who is very close to her, an intimate God who loves and frees her from the shackles of a patriarchal discourse. She knows Christ in a very personal way, so much so that Ignatius would have been proud of her. She speaks of the Son of God as one who has come to save and liberate her from the shackles of sin and death. Her songs and her language about God reflected in Jesus Christ are tangible and relate to her daily life. She may not possess a sophisticated theological education or hermeneutical tools for assessing the scriptures, yet she knows the Word of God from lived experience.

The God within enables women to relate to Jesus as the archetype of what the human species should be. This God begets life and nurtures it in love just as African women beget life in all its manifestations and nurture it in love in the most challenging circumstances imaginable. Unfortunately, this characteristic of

God as exhibited in Jesus escapes the imagination and interest of the male-dominated theology in Africa.

Thus, as the foregoing shows, for African women, one concrete manifestation of the creativity of the imagination emerges in how we name the sacred and the divine. This creativity bridges the gap between humanity and divinity and opens a doorway to the incomprehensible mystery of God. African women have myriad names for God, but the name they know most intimately in the depths of their being is God who loves. And we can imagine an infinite number of ways we encounter and experience this God, who loves selflessly and abundantly, in a kenosis flowing generously in and through the universe of love.

The image or the face of God reflected in African women is that of love; they love relentlessly and resiliently in acts that commit them to total self-giving. They know the God of love, and their lives flow from the God of love. It is futile to search for images to express this experience and reality of African women mirroring the mystery of the Divine. More than any image, it is an embodied experience that is easily distorted when pressed into antecedently fabricated patriarchal and androcentric categories or idols.

In exercising her power and gift of imagination, the African woman also experiences God as one who is in communion with all. She sees herself as a transmitter and promoter of life. She seeks not fame or power but the dignity that is accorded her and the rest of God's creation. She is very earthy and spirit led, and she frequently communicates with her God and ancestors living and dead. She is highly intuitive. She sees herself as a presence that is synonymous with life. She knows that she is brave and beautiful. Although some traditions fabricate negative images of her, she does not perceive herself in a negative light.

As I see it, the African woman shares an affinity with the prophetess of the Hebrew scriptures. Like Miriam, she raises her hands in praise and song and beats her tambourine. Like Deborah, she rouses the people to follow God's leading and inspires them to fulfill God's promises. Like Huldah, she reaches out to other women in compassion and support. The prophetic tradition has never been closed to women, albeit there have, at times, been struggles to preserve this understanding. This tradition comes alive in the spiritual experience of women in the exercise of the power and gift of imagination.

To conclude this excursus on the imaginative power and creativity of women's spirituality in an African context, I mention another analogous example I can draw on to illustrate the creativity, resilience, and fruitfulness of the power of imagination as exemplified by women and their practice of spirituality. Here again this example derives from my experience of spirituality as an African woman. Yet the key lesson is that the gift of the imagination is second nature to women.

THIS EARTH—OUR MOTHER

In many African cultures, the earth is a deity and is venerated as such. There are many reasons this is so. Essentially, the veneration of the earth is a recognition of its gift of abundant life and sustenance to humanity. In approaching this deity and in their prayers, supplication, praise, and worship, devotees imagine this deity as a mother first and foremost taking care of her children and deserving respect. They imagine all things emerging from her. They imagine her bringing balance, harmony, and fairness to human interaction and relationships. They imagine her as one who punishes those who hurt others. In the end, they imagine her as the one to whom all things return at the end of time. In my imagination, this earth, our mother, bears life and allows life to end when it is time. Consider this Akan (Ghana) prayer.

O Mother Earth we are fully dependent on you, it is you who receive us with your open arms at birth when we were yet naked. You supply our daily wants with your rich resources indeed you nurture us throughout our earthly life. And when the wicked death finally snatches us away, you will still be there to open up your womb and receive us all back.[2]

This prayer is a beautiful commentary on the African traditional way of perceiving the earth as our mother.

What makes this luxuriant, earthy, and relatable conception of the Divine possible is the gift and creativity of our imagination. The experience of naming God's activities resonates deeply with the interior disposition of African women. In their intuitiveness and incisive ability to be present in the world through love, they imagine God as active in ways beyond the controlling language of patriarchal theologizing. Their knowledge and understanding of God are simultaneously earthy and transcendent, personal and mystical.

Bereft of imagination, our prayers will be dry, empty, suffocating, and frustrating. From what I have experienced of Ignatian spirituality, imagination is the gift that waters and nourishes contemplative prayer and enables it to come alive and to flourish in the expansive universe of our senses. Perhaps the expression that comes closest to this insight is the Psalmist's exhortation "Taste and see that the Lord is good" (Ps 34:8).

IMAGINATION: OUR BEST-KEPT SECRET

The preceding section laid the theological foundation for the idea that the gift of imagination is a vital element for women who engage in the *Spiritual Exercises*. This foundation is theological; it doubles necessarily as a critique of social, cultural, and religious factors that impede the ability of women to tap into and deploy the gift of imagination to see that another world is possible; another God is possible in their moment of encounter with the Divine.

In chapter 3, I discussed the multiple wounds visited upon women by prejudices, biases, and stereotypes inspired by culture, religion, and society. When we consider deeply the dynamics of Ignatian spirituality, we discover that it is a powerful tool for imagining that another spiritual world is possible for women.

Considering the insidious and pervasive background of patriarchy, sexism, and discrimination, the woman who engages in the adventure of the *Spiritual Exercises* may never have had the freedom to use her imagination. Like many other women, she too may need to contend with a variety of obstacles to expressing herself and tell her story more freely. The words and rituals that she is accustomed to in various Christian traditions and faith traditions may not honor or reflect her feminine energy, power, or perception. Consequently, the woman of the *Exercises* may never have had a taste of what her mind can bring to birth through the gift of her imagination. She does not quite see her body, her mind, her whole being as the vessel and the domain of the Divine. She may not see herself as the channel of divine revelation and truth. Yet she can change, or rather transcend, these man-made obstacles by deploying the power of her imagination.

As evident in the preceding section, it is characteristic for women to be judged and undermined for their use of their imagination. But women have a way of circumventing such negative judgments. Thus, for example, in the Nigerian culture, a woman may pray for her children and imagine their futures and through her prayers project blessings on them. A prayer of her imagination could be verbalized to a child who is very kind to her parents. Drawing on her imagination, she might pray and tell the child that she or he will prosper in so many ways. She may pray that the child and those who take care of her will be successful in anything she touches, will live among kings and queens, and enjoy a fruitful life. In this moment and practice of prayer, the dominant means is her imagination, through which she encounters the Divine and by which the Divine is present to her.

The woman of the *Exercises* can benefit from imaginative contemplative prayer if encouraged and gently guided. Besides the prejudices of culture, society, and religion, one challenge that besets women in their exercise of spirituality is the dichotomy of the mind or intellect from the body and the imagination. I am alluding here to the so-called Cartesian divorce credited to the sixteenth-century French philosopher René Descartes. Undoubtedly, this philosophical approach that separates mind from body, humanity from nature, man from woman—in short, dualistic thinking—has created myriad challenges for spirituality. I desist from the temptation to provide an inventory of these challenges stemming from the divorce of the emotional from the physical, which range from climate change to economic inequalities. Suffice it to say that, in certain instances, this climate of dualism can be insidious and pervasive and hinder the human capacity to balance the multiple energies and gifts, especially the gift of the imagination, from entering a space of encounter with the Divine with one's entire being.

Understandably, the woman of the *Exercises* perhaps unconsciously has been subject to this separation of mind from emotions, analytical thinking from imaginative wanderings. As I see it, this woman will be enriched if she can discover and recover the gift of her imagination to see, feel, taste, smell, touch, and bring together her experiences to a place of consciousness where integration can occur between body, mind, spirit, and heart. In essence, through the agency of the *Spiritual Exercises*, she can move toward a wholeness of mind and spirit.

Such is the power and possibility inherent in the exercise of the imagination in Ignatian spirituality.

In chapter 3, we saw the multiple and rich possibilities that could constitute the background of the woman who embarks on the exhilarating journey of the *Spiritual Exercises*—painter, singer, baker, dancer, designer. In each of these instances, her imagination can create and open a new world of encounter with the God of her painting, her song, her bread, her dance, her creation.

Far from being a flight of fancy, her use of her imagination becomes a creative means for seeing and presenting herself as she really is before her God and seeing God in who she really is. In this sacred space of encounter and presence, she can imagine for example, the words and symbolisms of her poetry coming together like the dry bones of Ezekiel 37 and being breathed into life by the God who quickens her creativity into life. Or she could imagine the food she cooks and the different ingredients coming together or even imagine the groceries and household items she would like to buy before she gets to the store.

When we see things in this light, it becomes clear that the woman of the *Exercises* is anything but unimaginative. With the help of an astute and attentive spiritual companion, she is very capable of discovering the power and gift of her imagination and realizing that she is far more creative than she has even allowed herself to consider. The dualisms of our culture may have prevented her from acknowledging her depths and the creative recognition of her purpose, her being, her desires. Thankfully, she is stronger and more creative than the limits imposed on her by this culture of dualism.

Thus, through the doorways of her imagination, the woman of the *Exercises* can create images and experiences that reflect her most interior desires and longings for spiritual fulfillment. In her imagination, she can come much closer to the power in her to create the kind of world that is suitable for her and others' flourishing. In her imagination, she can engender images and feel the life and place she sees as hers. Using her imagination, the woman of the *Exercises* touches the essence of her being through images and songs and poetry and even through the unknown and hidden stories in her.

In the next chapter, I consider the importance of storytelling in the spiritual experience of women in relation to Ignatian spirituality. What is important for now is to recognize that by the gift and grace of her imagination, the woman of the *Exercises* cocreates a new world with the life-giving Spirit of the God who dwells in her. With the gift and grace of her imagination, she can perceive and come home to where God is in her. In and through her imaginative prayer, she can embrace her whole being in that place—her God-place—where she is totally immersed in the God-adventure. In this God-place, she is free to be herself; she can respond freely to the God of her desires and longing.

In this sacred place of contemplative imagination, the woman of the *Exercises* can experience life holistically. She becomes able to touch her being and recognize what belongs to her and what has been foisted on her by others. Through the gift of imagination, she can experience the harmony of all that is authentically hers, that is, every moment, encounter, experience, and activity that makes her fully alive.

In keeping with the Ignatian principle of finding God in all things, in her imaginative contemplative prayer, she can see the God who is present to her in all things, all peoples, all events, and all circumstances. Her heart will be moved to respond accordingly because her feelings have been quickened to life, her emotions have been animated, and all the images of her conscious and unconscious reality are now present to her. Gone is the unhealthy Cartesian divorce. Whether painful or joyful, no part of her experience is alien to her God. Through the gift of her imagination, she is at peace, at home, and in harmony with her God in a relationship in which she is encountering the livingness and abundance of She who Is.

I AM WONDERFULLY AND FEARFULLY MADE

At this point in our journey, I invite the reader to an experience of imaginative contemplation. As women, if we could deploy the gift and power of our imagination in contemplative prayer, what would it look like? To do this exercise, it is important to recall the four elements of the *Spiritual Exercises* that we noted in the preceding chapter: posture, composition of place, application of senses, and colloquy.

Find a conducive location and settle into a comfortable position. Take a few deep breaths. Through your senses, pay attention to your environment of surroundings. Become attuned to and in harmony with them. Recall Psalm 139: "I am fearfully and wonderfully made...."

Begin to imagine the wonder and awesomeness of your being. You are wonderful, and you are awesome. Imagine both qualities of your life and how God created you, this woman, at the beginning of time in the womb of God. Imagine God's response at the dawn of your creation: you are created whole and beautiful. Imagine and hear God's marvel at your stunning beauty..."She is very good!"

Imagine what your life is now. What has become of this *imago Dei* you were meant to be? Is this image broken, shattered, sullied? See this *imago Dei* in the many small pieces into which it has been shattered in your life. What caused this brokenness? In your imagination, pick up each piece and examine it closely...the pain and the sadness, the joy and the excitement. In your imagination, see in each small piece the face of God still smiling at you, still appreciating you, still marveling at your awesome beauty.

Imagine each of these small pieces coming together to make a whole. They are no longer scattered and strewn about. Together, they form a whole. Together, they form a wonderful and awesome creation. Together, they form you. Imagine yourself alive and whole again as the *imago Dei*. In the quiet of your heart, repeat the words of the Psalmist this time with gratitude. I thank you, God of my life, for making me so beautifully, wonderfully, and awesomely....

This exercise of imaginative contemplation was inspired by the First Week of the *Spiritual Exercises*. In chapter 2, we examined and questioned the applicability of the idea of a healthy sense of shame to women's experience. When Ignatius invites the retreatant to make a record of her or his sin and imagine the horror and putridness of her or his actions, the outcome could be overpowering and depressing. In one sense, Ignatius is asking the retreatant not only to imagine hell on earth but also to place herself or himself in that hell (*Spiritual Exercises*, 65–70).

As a woman, I see things differently. Or rather, I can imagine sinfulness and hell differently. I do not need fire and brimstone to imagine both. More important, in my imagination, God is never absent from the reality of sinfulness. Thus, as a woman approaching the First Week of the *Exercises*, my starting point is wholeness and beauty. I am indeed wonderfully and fearfully made. This *imago Dei* may be shattered and scattered by a variety of factors including my own limitations, but the God of my beauty and life is capable of gathering the pieces and— small piece by small piece—pulling these bits and shattered images together. In this sense, experiencing God's compassion and mercy is not a mechanical thing; rather, by the gift of my imagination, I experience grace and mercy being conferred on me and I experience God recreating the *imago Dei* that I am.

In my imagination, as we saw in the contemplative exercise above, through contemplative prayer, these small glimmers of images of the totality of my being come together again, quickened to life by the God of my life. I emerge from this moment of imaginative contemplation stronger and more whole, and the reflection of God's image in my life is clearer, sharper, and more intense. I recognize myself as I truly am in God: wonderfully and fearfully made, because I am the *imago Dei*.

As a spiritual companion to many women, I have discovered that not all women who embark on the journey of the *Spiritual Exercises* understand or even accept all they might be experiencing in imaginative contemplative prayer. To reiterate an important point in this book, in accompanying women in their imaginative contemplation, a requisite attitude or disposition is attentive and nonjudgmental listening, one that allows the spiritual companion to listen attentively and reverently to the woman of the *Exercises* in a mutual awareness of signs of the presence of Spirit in her story. It will be an unfolding story that might even look new or strange to her. In her prayer, surprises lurk, and she may be amazed by who and what appears. Yet she will recognize the presence of God that fills her imaginative contemplation as gentleness and tenderness, as mercy and compassion.

ENCOURAGING THE GIFT OF WOMAN'S IMAGINATION

The woman who engages in the wonderful journey of the *Spiritual Exercises* will benefit from using her imagination when engaged in contemplation, dialogue, and colloquy with the characters in the scriptures. As I mentioned, the attitude or disposition incumbent on the spiritual companion is attentive and reverent listening. What might a spiritual companion look out for—to recognize and to affirm—in the woman of the *Exercises*?

Considering what I have demonstrated so far, probably one of the possible manifestations in the woman of the *Exercises* is low self-esteem or self-doubt. Deploying her imagination to engage with the God who dwells in her might initially appear to be impossible. To journey with her reality, the spiritual companion needs to be sensitive to the scripture passages or texts from other sources that might attract such a person. For example, this could be texts that show Jesus going off to pray by himself and taking refuge from the pressure and demands of the crowds. This could be a safe space for her to place herself—a place of silence and of refuge. The woman of the *Exercises* might find herself attracted to this tired and challenged Jesus because his experience aligns with hers. She could just come and sit beside him as he prays in her imagination and in silence—both being present to each other.

It is also possible that the flurry of activities that occupies her time and space may prevent her from settling down, shutting out the noises, and engaging her gift of imagination. This is not unusual for women who have a thousand and one chores to attend to at the same time. The challenge then is for her to slow down, take a deep breath, and ready herself for meditation without feeling guilty. Rather than force her into silence, it might be helpful to invite her to imagine herself in front of Jesus and imagine him asking her, "What are you looking for? Who are you looking for?" (see John 1:38). This could be permission for her to say everything she has to say until she runs out of words, notices the person behind the question, and begins to engage with him with and in her whole being.

One gift of the imagination is that it is a call to a place of rest. The woman of the *Exercises* can create this space of rest and ready her heart to encounter her God. This is how I read Ignatius's suggestion that in approaching the time and place of prayer, the retreatant is to take a moment to prepare her or his heart for this moment of deep encounter: "I will raise my mind and think how God our Lord is looking at me" (*Spiritual Exercises*, 75). For until she is able to rest interiorly, the woman of the *Exercises* will find it difficult to place herself calmly with the God of her desires and longing.

In addition to low self-esteem, a challenge that may confront the woman of the *Exercises* is that of living with a false image of herself. She may appear in charge—a woman who must be right and who commands what happens around her. To come to a place of silence, rest, and trust requires much patience and understanding. In this instance, it could be helpful to invite her to use her imagination to engage scripture texts or moments when the woman takes the initiative in the presence of Jesus of Nazareth such as the mother of the sick child who insisted that Jesus accede to her request to heal her child (Matt 15:21–28). Through patient encounter, dialogue, and colloquy, she would begin to see that the healing of her child does not depend on her insistence, but is a gift of the tenderness and mercy of her God. She does not need to fall into the trap of dominating the situation and controlling the outcome as she has been used to in the patriarchal world of her experience. It is enough for her to show up and allow the God of her desires and longing to touch her vulnerability with tenderness and transform her false image into the truth and beauty of who she truly is—the *imago Dei*.

Finally, it is possible that the woman of the *Exercises* desires to engage with the risen Christ. Yet it may be that her multiple traumas make it difficult for her to set aside the various things weighing her down and preventing her from reaching the depths and fullness of her wonderful and awesome being. Without ruling out the necessity of seeking help in a professional setting before she can fully engage with the *Spiritual Exercises*, she will benefit from support to answer some of the desires and longings of her heart. For this woman, her imagination may well be too active, and she can still graphically recall her traumas. Without dismissing them or her, she may be helped to imagine how Jesus Christ truly desires to comfort, heal, and transform those experiences into spiritual strengths. Much discernment is required for this situation.

A GUIDED MEDITATION

This chapter has been about the gift of the imagination, one of the best-kept secrets waiting to be discovered by women in the *Spiritual Exercises*. To conclude this reflection, I invite the reader to an imaginative exercise using a rather unorthodox means, namely, the lyrics of a familiar hymn, a poem, or even the timeless song, "Imagine," by John Lennon. This task should not surprise us. Remember that Ignatius did not shy away from using the Basque songs and dances he learned from his adoptive mother, Maria de Garin, to embellish and enrich the experience of the *Spiritual Exercises*!

In fact, this exercise is akin to a method of prayer that Ignatius recommends in the *Spiritual Exercises* that "consists in contemplating the meaning of each word of a prayer"; the person reflects on one word at time and continues "to consider the word as long as meanings, comparisons, relish, and consolations connected with it are found" (*Spiritual Exercises*, 249–57).

Find and settle into a comfortable space and position. Take a few deep breaths and allow your body to relax. Attune and align all your senses to your surroundings and environment.

Begin to read slowly the lyrics stopping each time something strikes your imagination…. For example:

> *You may imagine a world where there is no heaven…*
> *You may imagine that everyone is living for today…*
> *You may imagine a world where people have lost all*
>   *hope.*

Then you may imagine a world where everyone lives in peace...
A world where there are no possessions and people are sharing all that they have...
Finally, you may imagine a world that comes together as one.

Conclude this imaginative exercise by sharing your thoughts with God, your dreams, and your heart's longings and desires. Tell God all the things you imagine yourself saying to God at this moment in your life.

5

The God-Place of Storytelling

Until the lioness learns to write, the story of the hunt will always glorify the hunter.

—An African proverb

Growing up in Nigeria, I was always intrigued by the popular pastime of storytelling. Fortunately, the nature of my father's occupation necessitated our family's occasional relocation to various parts of the country. This occupational and geographical mobility stimulated my interest in stories from diverse cultures. Highly anticipated visits with my grandmother especially offered me the opportunity to revel in the enchanted world of storytelling.

Typically, children gathered around adults or among themselves and listened to stories. The genre was varied—from legends to fables, from riddles to myths. But each contained a lesson for life. Interestingly, the storyteller appropriated a certain narrative license that doubled as narrative power. She or he could embellish the story or introduce a new slant to guarantee a particular outcome. This was not manipulation; rather, it was license and creativity combined to enhance the authority of the narrator and the pertinence of the story's moral or message.

Storytelling was an inclusive exercise involving women and men, albeit women gathered with their folk and men congregated with theirs. Unlike other aspects of life, storytelling was subjected to neither gender policing nor gendered cultural sanctions.

In the previous chapter, I emphasized the gift and the power of the imagination as an essential element or component of Ignatian spirituality in its expression in the *Spiritual Exercises*. Construed as a gift, imagination recreates an encounter with and places us in the vicinity of the Divine. Thanks to this gift, women can subvert and transcend barriers imposed by patriarchal penchants in culture, religion, and society.

Building on the discussion of the gift of imagination, in this chapter, we explore one of the correlates of the application and use of this gift, namely, storytelling. My main point contains multiple aspects. As mentioned in the introductory paragraph, what enabled storytellers in my childhood experience to shape and embellish the narrative was their imagination. Second, an authentic spiritual exercise is hardly divorced from our experience or even from our stories. I recall the themes of finding God in all things and the idea of embodiment I have presented and explored in preceding chapters.

Third, storytelling confers agency, power, and confidence on the narrator. For "until the lioness learns to write, the story of the hunt will always glorify the hunter." Storytelling is a means for reclaiming one's voice. As a woman, I consider this a priceless gift.

In this chapter, I will underscore the importance of women creating and sharing their personal stories as part of how they deploy and apply the gift of their imagination to prayer. Women's stories can become a sacred space for encounter with the

Divine. My experience of the *Spiritual Exercises* has convinced me that it invites the process and exercise of storytelling.

Composition of place is about creating your own narrative, as is the application of the senses. When the woman of the *Exercises* can create and tell her stories in the presence of the God of her life, the outcome can be life-changing. Such an experience can lead women to discover sparks of the Spirit through an imaginative and holistic awareness of how God is present and active in their stories.

THE FOUNDATION OF OUR STORYTELLING

The *Spiritual Exercises* is founded on scripture. As originally conceived, outlined, and structured by Ignatius, the *Exercises* opens a pathway to scripture. The engagement and openness to scripture is neither gratuitous nor perfunctory. The person making the *Exercises* does not take the scripture at face value. She or he is not expected to be exegetically literate; Ignatius presents scripture as stories and events in the life of Christ. There is a narrative quality to them that allows the retreatant to enter their dynamics as an active participant. Again, this narrative quality recalls what we saw in the previous chapter about the gift and power of the imagination.

From my experience as a woman approaching the *Spiritual Exercises*, this narrative or storied approach is important for various reasons. First, scripture is a common source of reference for those who authoritatively claim to speak on behalf of women or to define the nature and place of women in church and society. The patriarchal pastime of putting women in their place easily but erroneously seeks and claims justification in scripture. When I approach scripture through the lens of the *Spiritual Exercises*, I can recover something akin to the narrative license and narrative power of my childhood experience of storytelling; no longer am I compelled to accept one biased or prejudiced viewpoint. In the gift of my imagination, I can compose the sacred place and story of my encounter with the God of my life and apply the entire range of my senses to this encounter to render it an intensely personal and sumptuously fulfilling experience.

The second point is that, as mentioned, even a retreatant who considers herself or himself theologically unschooled and lacking the tools of critical interpretation of biblical resources and traditions can easily acquire the tool needed to access scripture so that it is spiritually satisfying; that tool is precisely the combination of storytelling and the gift of imagination.

The third point concerns the double-sided nature of the authority of scripture. Just as scriptural authority has been used to demean and undermine the dignity of women in some instances, the *Spiritual Exercises* offers women an opportunity to achieve the opposite—to affirm and honor their intrinsic worth and inalienable dignity in the sacred place of encounter with the God of their lives. The devices Ignatius built into the *Spiritual Exercises* such as composition of place, colloquy, and application of senses are apt for intentionally and creatively recreating and retelling the vast array of biblical stories. As I have mentioned repeatedly, this act of recreation is hardly an impersonal experience.

In the *Spiritual Exercises*, we are drawn into the biblical story by the application of our senses. We become active participants capable of shaping and influencing the outcome of the story. This does not mean we control or manipulate the stories; it simply means that the events, people, and places of the stories are no longer alien to us. Better still, our own stories are no longer alien to the biblical stories. Our active participation through the gift of our imagination opens the way to fresh meanings and a fuller experience of the God of our lives.

The beauty of women telling their own stories is that it creates a space for displaying our giftedness. We do not need others to construct or tell our stories for us. We have our own voices, and we can speak; we have experiences that are unique to us, that only we as women can narrate. The qualities of our narrative imagery and symbolism derive from the depths of our being as women. They are valid, significant, life-affirming, and antithetical to the fixation on the biological and the patriarchal domination of women.

As the woman of the *Exercises* reads and rereads scripture, she receives permission to generate her own stories and narratives. The agency and power in this process enables her to enter more deeply the sacred space of encounter with the God of her life. No longer are Old and New Testament stories told about her or despite her. She can become the author of these stories; and she is empowered to integrate her own stories into these stories.

In the *Spiritual Exercises*, when Ignatius invites the retreatant to identify, name, and express the graces that she or he desires, it is an invitation to tell our stories—stories about our joys and hopes, our pain and anguish, our struggles and troubles, and our dying and living. There is no more poignant example than that of Hannah recapping her story for the benefit of a male religious functionary who misjudged her as a drunk whereas she was pouring out her heart and soul before her God: "Sir, I have not drunk any wine or beer," she corrected Eli politely. "I am deeply troubled, and I was telling the LORD about all my problems. Don't think I am a bad woman. I have been praying so long because I have so many troubles and am very sad" (see 1 Sam 1:15–16). Again, it is for this reason that the combination of the gift of imagination and the exercise of storytelling is profoundly refreshing and liberating for the woman of the *Exercises*.

The trio of religion, culture, and society has always been slow to listen to women's stories and narratives and consider them credible, authentic, and valid. This pathological condition of ecclesiastical, cultural, and societal deafness is more than regrettable; it is outright dangerous. Besides, it appears as a form of deafness to what the Spirit is saying to the church (see Rev 2:29). The tendency to write women out of history, silence their voices, or misrepresent their true desires and values violates and mutilates the integrity of the body of Christ.

WOMEN'S STORIES IN THE *SPIRITUAL EXERCISES*

In my experience of accompanying women on their journey of the *Spiritual Exercises*, I am amazed at the variety, quality, and depths of the stories they bring to the experience, or rather that the experience of the *Exercises* unlocks in them, often in ways that they never saw themselves capable of experiencing.

As I wrote earlier, countless women played key roles in influencing and shaping Ignatian spirituality. To return to one foundational moment, consider as an example the songs and dances that Maria de Garin, the blacksmith's wife, taught Iñigo as a child, which became important tools for leading other people into the journey of the *Spiritual Exercises*. Who would have thought of such a genial element of Ignatian spirituality? It would not be pure speculation to suggest that she told him stories too.

In chapter 1, we considered Hugo Rahner's collection of letters between Ignatius and his women friends through which they offered help to one another. We always need to be aware of the vital role women played in the shaping of the *Exercises* for us to appreciate its relevance to our lives. Perhaps for some, this aspect of Ignatius's journey may seem trivial and immaterial, but from my experience of spiritual accompaniment, the more I think about it and reflect on it, the more I am convinced that there is a kindred spirit between the *Exercises* and women and Ignatian spirituality in general even today. The reason for this spiritual kinship is the formative role that women played in Ignatius's upbringing and in his spiritual development.

The woman of the *Exercises* is a bundle and composite of lived realities, desires, dreams, journeys, and especially stories. All these areas of her life come together uniquely in the last of these—stories. As I mentioned above, storytelling is second nature for many African women. The award-winning Nigerian novelist Chimamanda Ngozi Adichie once said,

> Stories matter. Many stories matter. Stories have been used to dispossess and to malign, but stories can also be used to empower and to humanize. Stories can break the dignity of a people, but stories can also repair that broken dignity.[1]

This is precisely my point.

As I pointed out in my discussion of the characteristics of biblical stories, what Adichie is saying is that stories are a double-edged sword; they can enrich life, and they can diminish life. Isn't this the story of women's lives in so many parts of the world? As part of this amorphous collective called minorities, women's stories have been missing. In fact, it isn't that women's stories have been missing; rather, others have told our stories—others have impersonated women's voices and told stories about us that mostly define us in our biological roles and relationships to men as mothers, wives, sisters, and so on, but not stories of our deep friendships as women working and journeying lovingly with one another. Again, "Until the lioness learns to write, the story of the hunt will always glorify the hunter."

The *Spiritual Exercises* is a space for women to compose and tell their own stories. Evidently, women have not always been free to create, own, tell, and celebrate their stories with confidence outside of the norms imposed by religion, culture, and society. The woman of the *Exercises* could well be one such woman bursting with stories she has never been able or allowed to tell.

Another African proverb states, "One falsehood spoils a thousand truths." In my experience as a spiritual companion to many women, the woman who commits herself to the adventure of the *Exercises* is a woman of many stories. Her stories are pearls of great value. They may not always be polished and refined, but that is not the point. In fact, she herself is a story—an untold story, a hidden story shrouded in silence and unable to share her profound experiences of who she is in and before God.

In my ministry of spiritual companionship, I have encountered several women who have never touched and owned the stories of who they were called to be, the beauty and gifts of who they were, the journeys of their lives and all their desires and dreams, joys and hopes, pains and anxieties, longings and aspirations. In this context, one of the greatest discoveries or gifts is that although the woman of the *Exercises* may have a voice that has been muted by a myriad of things, she has a beautiful soul; she has a story deep in her being that is yearning to be known, heard, and celebrated.

As noted in our discussion of the woundedness and fear of women's bodies in chapter 3, she might be feeling unclean and unworthy of life and love because of the many stories that have been told about her. Because she has not been able to tell the story of her life, she probably has never been able to tell of the wonders of who God is for her. Fortunately, as Ignatius says in the *Exercises*, in this space, she is now capable of seeking and being empowered to seek the divine will in her life. Once she enters the space of the *Exercises*, she becomes aware of her desires to discover what God desires for her in her particular and fundamental story, the story that gives meaning to her life or what Ignatius would call her "Principle and Foundation."

I believe that without creating, sharing, and celebrating her story, the woman of the *Exercises* may never touch the depths of who God is for her. Sharing her story is the same thing as finding God alive and active in her life.

It is important to pay attention to how she feels about telling her story. Is she afraid perhaps that her story isn't good enough? Does she doubt that others will believe it? Is she worried that others might even dismiss it? How does she feel about her story? This is a point of great sensitivity, especially for people who are privileged to be spiritual companions to the woman of the *Exercises*.

Attention, sensitivity, and reverence are vital dispositions and attitudes on the part of a spiritual companion encountering this woman. The former bears the solemn responsibility of praying for and seeking the grace not to silence her voice and mute her story yet again just like the rest of culture, religion, and society has tended to do; the grace of patience to wait, to listen deeply, and to be focused and attentive to the gentle ways that God is being revealed in and through her story.

In her adventure of the *Spiritual Exercises*, the woman of the *Exercises* is hoping to encounter her God in her own story, discover her own truths, and appreciate her own experiences. She may not realize it, but from an Ignatian perspective, her story is the *main* ingredient for God's intervention in and through the *Exercises*. She has come to the God-place opened by the *Spiritual Exercises* to share her story, trusting that she will find a receptive and welcoming heart as she yearns to discover how her God is shaping and reshaping her through her story.

"One falsehood spoils a thousand truths." The inability for women's stories to be heard and celebrated has spoiled thousands of the truths of humanity's reflection of the *imago Dei*. If the woman of the *Exercises* has experienced not being allowed to tell her story, she is probably like the "caged bird" in Maya Angelou's poem whose "wings are clipped and...feet are tied," who "sings with a fearful trill" but "sings of freedom." She may come to the *Exercises* from a society, a religion, or a community that does not consider her story worthy of modeling the image and experience of God. All she knows is his-story, not her-story. Consequently, she might not understand that her unique life and story are part of the larger picture that is incomplete without them. She might have been abused, molested, and condemned; she might feel alienated from her own story. Yet her story is not every woman's story; her story is unique and without parallel. From my experience, the *Spiritual Exercises* offers a key to unleash her freedom, her beauty, and her uniqueness in front of her God.

In the presence of this woman of the *Exercises*, the spiritual companion must listen with humility and reflect with honesty and truth: Do I have ears large enough to hear her story? Do I have a heart deep enough to bear her story? Is my presence inviting and still enough to enable the woman in front of me to discover and recover her voice to tell her story like no other?

TRYING OUT MY VOICE

I invite the reader to engage in an exercise that brings some of the foregoing considerations closer to home. For this exercise, take your mind back to the story of Jesus and the Samaritan woman at the well in John 4:1–42 or any other story of Jesus's encounter with women in the New Testament.

Jesus encounters this woman at a well. She is the woman in front of Jesus. But she is no ordinary woman; her troubles are legion. She has many falsehoods going against her—her ethnicity, her marital status, and her religious beliefs. Add to that her gender, which is her greatest obstacle. In short, her story is complicated, such that it is a scandal for a Jewish man to publicly initiate a conversation with her.

Find a conducive space and assume a comfortable position.

Take a few deep breaths and become attuned to your surroundings or environment with all your senses....

Imagine yourself at the same well standing in front of Jesus. Let Jesus notice you and notice him in return. Do not say a word. Let Jesus's gaze settle on you and yours on him.

Slowly and with much attention, begin to read the story of the unnamed Samaritan woman. As you read, note any aspect that connects to, resonates with, or resembles your story. If something strikes you, slow down, stay with it. When you eventually get to the end of the story, look at Jesus and using these words, speak to him.

> I come with my story
> I come with my uniqueness
> I come with my longing
> I come with my song
> I come with my truth
> I come with my desires
> I come with my pain
> I come with my healing
> I come with my fears
> I come with my hope
> I come with my troubles
> I come with all I am
> I come with my unfolding story
> I come to embrace my wholeness

Again, fix your gaze on Jesus and allow him to fix his on you. Listen to Jesus speaking to you. What is he saying to you?

THE PRINCIPLE AND FOUNDATION

The Spiritual Exercises begins with what Ignatius calls "The Principle and Foundation."

God created human beings to praise, reverence, and serve God, and by doing this, to save their souls.

God created all other things on the face of the earth to help fulfill this purpose.

From this it follows that we are to use the things of this world only to the extent that they help us to this end, and we ought to rid ourselves of the things of this world to the extent that they get in the way of this end.

For this it is necessary to make ourselves indifferent to all created things as much as we are able, so that we do not necessarily want health rather than sickness, riches rather than poverty, honor rather than dishonor, a long rather than a short life, and so in all the rest, so that we ultimately desire and choose only what is most conducive for us to the end for which God created us. (*Spiritual Exercises*, 23)[2]

People familiar with the *Exercises* may be surprised that I am introducing the Principle and Foundation in the final part of chapter 5. Am I not getting it wrong? Perhaps. As the expression suggests, it has to do with beginning or origin, the basis, the rationale. This is certainly how Ignatius intended it. I have a valid reason for saving this gem of the *Exercises* until now. But I do not intend to displace it from its original position. Bear in mind that this book is not the *Spiritual Exercises* and does not replace it. As I see it, the Ignatian Principle and Foundation is the foundational story, a narrative of origins just like the narratives of origins in Genesis. Because I am discoursing on the importance of storytelling in women's spirituality and particularly Ignatian spirituality, this is the natural and logical place to introduce and consider the Ignatian Principle and Foundation as a story of origins. To get a sense of how foundational this story of origins is from the point of view of women approaching the *Spiritual Exercises*, I offer a few considerations.

HER STORY IS...

One of the critical insights of Ignatius we find in the *Exercises* is the liberating idea that where God wants to lead the retreatant is more important than where the spiritual companion wants her or him to go. That is why, for example, Ignatius tells spiritual companions that their primary role is to get out of the way, not to interpose or intrude (*Spiritual Exercises*, 15). Rather, spiritual companions are to stand by like the pointer on a scale in equilibrium and allow God to relate personally with the woman of the *Exercises* and allow her to tell her story, not anybody else's story.

In the *Spiritual Exercises*, the Principle and Foundation is not a particular kind of meditation or contemplation. Ignatius calls it a consideration, that is, something to ponder, think about, and wonder about over and over. It is a repetitive exercise on the woman's identity as God's unique creation. As a woman approaching the *Exercises*, I find this reflective exercise to be a special gift to women precisely because of its nature as an enabler of their storytelling. Given its strategic location at the beginning of the *Exercises*, I consider it a powerful means for inviting women to create, own, and tell their stories as unique creations made in the image and likeness of God.

It would not be an exaggeration to think of the Principle and Foundation as the story of the *imago Dei*. In a profoundly challenging sense, it answers the questions Why am I here? What is my purpose? What is my story? Imagine what a gift it would be for the woman of the *Exercises* to be able to craft, articulate, and consider her story and purpose as part of God's creation story. It could become the occasion for her to discover many things about her life, her journey, and her purpose—like how God is still actively creating and recreating her, how she is experiencing her life in God, how God is filling her with the goodness of life, and how she is coming alive and being renewed. Sadly, it could also be a reminder of the dark side of her story, of how she is sometimes abused, exploited, and violated.

... A STORY OF THE *IMAGO DEI*

Seeing the Principle and Foundation as enabling the story of the woman of the *Exercises* is a powerful invitation for her to focus on the uniqueness and core of her being as the *imago Dei*. To discover this core, this center, and this meaning that makes her who she is—unique and unrepeatable—could be a special gift and invitation for her to come home to her own experience and story and to articulate them freely. As her story, the Principle and Foundation of the woman of the *Exercises* is what makes her a person like no other in the heart of a loving God, where her life is being molded and remolded, and her story is being born and reborn.

In fact, this is an invitation for her to see her story as an unfolding reality of the creator who is revealing Godself in her particular story. It is an unfinished story; better still, a never-ending story.

When I imagine the woman of the *Exercises* becoming able to see her life as a story being told by God, I get excited. How exciting that would be—God as the author of her story lovingly creating, shaping, narrating, and embellishing her story with love, tenderness, and compassion! Her story becomes a story of unending and undying love, never finished and always new.

... GOD'S STORY OF HER

When we imagine the Principle and Foundation as God's story of the woman of the *Exercises*, the opening lines might resemble the words of Jeremiah: "Before I formed you in the womb I knew you, and before you were born I consecrated you" (Jer 1:5), or of Isaiah: "I have called you by name, you are mine" (Isa 43:1), or of Hosea: "When you were a child, I loved you" (see Hos 11:1). When she sees her life as a story created and fashioned and told by God, her story changes; it becomes a bit like the prayer of St. Francis of Assisi: "Where there was a feeling of unworthiness, there will be a story of unending love and goodness; where there was self-deprecation, there will be a story of beauty and kindness; where there was diminishment, there will be a story of blossoming and flourishing!"

This is an exciting and refreshing approach. It is life changing for the woman of the *Exercises* to discover and recover her story—to compose, articulate, and celebrate her own Principle and Foundation. This experience could be truly liberating for her because she is no longer just any or every woman; she is this woman here and now to whom God is revealing God's self as love beyond all telling, the God who knows her and to whom she has bared her soul. She does not have to be somebody else to discover herself just as Ignatius could not be St. Francis or St. Dominic. Now, she knows that she has a story, that she is a story told by God, and that she is ready and able to retell her story in her own voice exactly the way God has created her story for praise, reverence, and fulfillment. Rather than beginning with the words "We are created...," she begins her story with her name as God knows and calls her: "I, Lola, am created..."

For the spiritual companion called to accompany this woman of the *Exercises*, it would also help to step back for a moment and reflect on oneself. Our ability to see, have compassion for, and understand this woman will be greatly affected by our own life stories. To hear and honor her story without undue interference, it is necessary to reflect on our own life patterns.

Depending on what has happened to us and with us in our lives, we will have greater or lesser empathy for her. If she has suffered abuse from a spouse or experienced an incestuous relationship with one of the men in her family, or rape, it is important to consider what the triggers are for us in our own lives. We may have had such experiences ourselves. Perhaps we had a parent who did not pay attention to us; perhaps we had a sibling who was preferred by our parents; or perhaps we had trouble in school and wanted to drop out. These kinds of reflections will help us pay attention to our own stories and thus avoid projecting them on the story of the woman of the *Exercises*.

The woman of the *Exercises* can tell her story freely and openly only if we have deeply and profoundly reflected on our own stories. I stress this point because if she (without her realizing it) touches something that makes us uncomfortable, she may know it, and it may skew the relationship of spiritual companionship. As spiritual companions, we ourselves must be at home with our own stories.

... HER

This perspective reveals that the woman who makes the pilgrimage of the *Spiritual Exercises* does not just have a story to be told. In a real sense, she is a story longing to be told, a story created by God. When she is able to tell her own experience as the *imago Dei* called forth into existence by God, she will gradually begin to come home to herself and discover her purpose of praise, reverence, service, and flourishing as in the Principle and Foundation. Again, when I look at my experience of making the *Spiritual Exercises* and accompanying other women as a spiritual companion, I am struck by the transformation that happens.

Once the woman of the *Exercises* has discovered her story in this way, the rest is a footnote; she can discern for herself what helps her fulfill her purpose in life and what hinders it. She can cultivate the gift of indifference that will allow her to realize what is at the center of her life and what distractions exist on the periphery of her life. She can begin to choose and act only insofar as her choices and actions deepen and expand her faith, love, and hope. She can exercise her freedom to desire and to choose only those stories that lead her into the depths of God's unconditional love for her and reject those that hinder this love. She can tell stories of where God dwells in her life as a friend, and she can begin to see everything about her life in a new light—in God's light, beauty, and goodness. She can see that God is creating and recreating and restoring everything in her life and about her life as uniquely her own. In discovering her story, she becomes aware of the fact that to praise, reverence, and serve God, she does not have to be anything other than herself. This is her story, and her story is her. This is the song of her soul and what brings her home to herself.

ANOTHER EXAMINATION OF CONSCIENCE

Something in this experience of a woman telling her own story is like the Examination of Conscience (*Spiritual Exercises*, 24) but not in the traditional way of looking for fault, failures, and failings and ridding oneself of them. In keeping with what we noted in chapter 2, the Examination of Conscience is a way the woman of the *Exercises* can begin to discard all the false stories that have been told about her, told for her, and told against her. She can start letting go of all that diminishes her life. She can now tell her authentic story. She knows it is not a perfect story, but her quest is not for perfection. She desires and longs to find herself and to come home to herself in praise, reverence, and service. Everything that gets in the way of this yearning is sinful.

The woman of the *Exercises* is a pilgrim. As noted in chapter 1, Ignatius, himself a pilgrim, composed the *Exercises* as a pathway to God. Likewise, the woman engaged in the Ignatian adventure is on a journey to self-discovery, self-awareness, and is always pondering, discerning, and contemplating the actions and presence of God in her life. For her to come home to herself, she must be able to tell her story as a revelation of who God is for her, in her, and with her. This takes time; it is a pilgrimage of a lifetime. The beauty of the *Spiritual Exercises* is that it offers her the God-place to begin this journey with confidence and joy.

MODES OF STORYTELLING

I will recap here how the woman of the *Exercises* can be enabled to tell her own story. Clearly, there are many modes of storytelling and sources of stories. A Zimbabwean proverb says, "If you can talk, you can sing. If you can walk, you can dance." Women can talk, sing, walk, and dance. These too are modes of composing, choreographing, and telling our stories.

In this and the previous chapter, I have referenced the practice of composition of place that Ignatius recommends in the *Exercises*. How do you make a composition of place? Without repeating the points already made, it is quite simple; you do so by "imagining the place" and making it as real and vivid as possible in all its details (*Spiritual Exercises*, 47). Ignatius says that we should see the place "with the eyes of the imagination" (*Spiritual Exercises*, 91); we are to imagine and recreate the scene of meditation and contemplation. To reiterate the point noted in chapter 4, this invitation to be imaginative constitutes the key for the woman of the *Exercises* to unlock her latent stories, her hidden stories, her untold stories.

But storytelling is not just about words and texts. Far from it. Ignatius invites the retreatant to use the imagination to see the place even to the point of imagining herself standing in the presence of God with all the angels and saints. I consider Ignatius's invitation a license or permission to undertake an audacious exercise of the imagination. How high and wide can her imagination be? How bold and audacious can her imagination be?

Recall the note in chapter 4 about using poetry, prose, nature, movement, song, and so on, as ways of opening her heart to God's love and presence in her life. Besides, the story of God's creation is not just about words. Pope John Paul II once said that creation was God's precious book but written with a multitude of created things that fill up the universe.[3]

When the *Spiritual Exercises* invites the woman of the *Exercises* to open the eyes of her imagination, it is an invitation to deploy her imagination to the fullest and without borders or boundaries. It is an invitation to create, narrate, and celebrate her story—to be a painter, a singer, a dancer, a knitter, a designer, an architect, a builder, a baker....The possibilities are limitless. In the spirit of the Ignatian tradition, there is no story without the imagination. There is even no prayer without the imagination. Imagination is the birthplace of story, the font of prayer, especially for women.

When we approach the *Spiritual Exercises* with a generous heart and a creative spirit (*Spiritual Exercises*, 5), we realize that Ignatius is giving us license to tell our stories using all the gifts and graces God has given us. This is particularly liberating, renewing, and refreshing for the woman of the *Exercises* whose story has previously been distorted or muted. She no longer needs to imagine or compose a story that has been prefabricated for her; she needs only to use her imagination to compose her story—her Principle and Foundation.

The woman of the *Exercises* may be just like the unnamed Samaritan woman in John with a discredited story, a victim of multiple forms of discrimination and abuse in her faith community, culture, and society. But while she was standing in front of Jesus at the well, he invited her to reclaim, tell, and own her story.

Notice the richness of her story. It is not just about multiple failed marriages; it is more about her deep faith, her theological acumen, and her rebellion against where society has placed her as a woman. Yet Jesus never condemned her; he invited her. He never dismissed her; he affirmed her. He never undermined her; he empowered her to lead others to God. This encounter transformed her life. At that point, she could see her life, her journey, her struggles, and her giftedness in a new light. She found her voice and exclaimed with joy, "Wow! You're a prophet? Could you be the Messiah? Hey everybody, come and see!"

Just like Jesus in the Samaritan woman's story, spiritual companions are to be ready to open the space in which the woman of the *Exercises* can recover and tell her story about the liberating love of God without feeling intimidated or shy about using her voice to do so. It entails encouraging her to own and use her voice and not be silenced or cowed by false stories told about her by others so that like the woman at the well, she can go forth with freedom and be loved and known for who she is, and praise, reverence, and serve God with her life.

A GUIDED MEDITATION

I invite readers to take part in an exercise that draws on insights in this chapter. It is a simple exercise that invites you to tell your stories as only you can.

Find a conducive place and settle into a comfortable position. Take a few deep breaths. Pay attention to all your senses, and align them with your surroundings, your environment. Imagine yourself in God's celestial court, in the presence of God and surrounded by all the angels and saints. Gradually step up and as if making a statement, say with confidence and boldness,

> Dear God, I am [your name], the woman you created
> with love and hold with love. You are the love of my

life and the God of my love. You fashioned me in my mother's womb, and I was born on this day...in the month of...and in the year of....In my creaturehood, I embody your infinite love as your work of art. Like my sister, Miriam, here present, I raise my voice in songs of praise, and like Mary, here present, I am a woman of truth, beauty, and love. Everything and anything in my life is a gift of your love enabling me to become fully the woman you created and continue to create in me.

By the grace of your love, I open my heart to all your creatures, including women, my own kind, and men, the opposite kind, as a part of my reverence to you, the God and love of my life. Emboldened by your love, I refuse to embrace or honor any creature, power, institution, system, or structure that claims to be you or acts as you. I will rise up to my full self against all hindrances set in my way by culture, religion, and society. I will rise up as the equal creature made by you. I will invite the other kind to learn from me about how to care for and carry the earth in the womb of love.

As a woman, like Mary, the mother of Jesus, I dwell in the center of the circle of life. I carry life in me as I dwell in your womb of love where you, O God, are birthing and creating, renewing and transforming, and where everything is unfolding, be it sickness, health, wealth, fame, recognition, long life, short life— all that is still to come. My being is the place where love meets love. I desire to be there in the womb of your love and be fashioned into your dreams for me.

Continue your address to God and to God's heavenly court. When you are satisfied, pause and listen to God's response to your unique Principle and Foundation.

6

Contemplative Awakening, Awareness, and Action

A woman is never old when it comes to the dance she knows.

—An African proverb

In the last five chapters, we have explored various themes of Ignatian spirituality using the *Spiritual Exercises* as its concrete and comprehensive expression. The foundational idea is the affinity between Ignatian spirituality and women. The idea stems from my deep and personal conviction that women played key roles in the life of St. Ignatius of Loyola—from his infancy to the founding of the Society of Jesus and beyond. Based on this conviction, I have offered a new perspective on how women are and can become at home with the profoundly enriching, renewing, and transformative dynamics of this treasure of Ignatian spirituality. Aspects of these dynamics include finding God in all things, embodiment, imagination, and storytelling.

This idea of affinity is close to my heart. In advancing it, I am reminded to reiterate that women are not mere recipients of Ignatian spirituality; women and the *Spiritual Exercises* are not strange bedfellows. On the contrary, just as women shaped its origins, women who engage in the *Spiritual Exercises* continue to shape its progress and adaptability in their lives. We must never forget that. Ignatian spirituality creates a God-place for women to identify, nurture, and express their desires and longings for the God of their lives.

In discussing the ideas of embodiment and imagination in chapters 3 and 4, I underlined the importance of feelings, emotions, body, and self in the spiritual journey of the woman of the *Exercises*. I emphasized the embodied nature of prayer and imaginative contemplation for women because the woman who engages in the *Exercises* does so holistically. She comes as she is and brings who she is in her entirety to this graced experience. And as we saw in the preceding chapter, who she is *is* her story.

CONTEMPLATIVES IN ACTION

In this chapter, I explore some aspects of what it means to be a contemplative in action and to encounter the fullness of God in all creation every moment of our existence and why these matter to the woman of the *Exercises*.

First, let us think about the meaning of the word *contemplative*. What comes to your mind when you think of it?

Ignatian spirituality entails a mystical inclusiveness. In it, nothing is considered insignificant. Our stories and desires, our bodies and ourselves, and our imagination and dreams—everything becomes a privileged and graced place of and a space for prayer. God desires to encounter us in all things. Considering this mystical inclusiveness, being contemplative is being deeply in touch with the source of all being with all our being. It matters less how we define or what or whom we recognize as this source and more that we allow ourselves into that place and space of encounter as we are.

Being in touch with the source of all being or with the Divine does not immobilize or paralyze us. Instead, this exhilarating experience energizes us and calls us forth to embody the presence and energy of the Divine in our lives—in our choices and decisions, and our actions and responses. Seen in this light, contemplation is hardly ever a disincarnate or disembodied exercise; it is deeply connected with action. In Ignatian spirituality, there is never one without the other.

Let us think of ourselves as contemplatives in the making. From this perspective, as we have seen repeatedly, the woman of the *Exercises* is on a path of discovering her deepest self through her daily choices that reflect her longing and desire to be one with her God every moment. By doing so, she is gradually coming home to herself in her sacred space or in her God-place. I have always found it a privilege as a spiritual companion to be present and attentive to her journey of discernment of God's presence and actions in her daily living.

The Birth of a Contemplative

In my journey with Ignatian spirituality, I have often wondered how Ignatius came to see God in all things. How did this soldier-turned-saint come home to himself, to his sacred space, to his God-place? I believe Ignatius took the path of contemplation. By his own account and the account of those who knew him, nothing escaped his attention, be it his dreams or daydreaming, his stargazing or pilgrimage, his scruples or discernment, the good and the bad spirits as he was wont to call them.

He cultivated and possessed an incredibly heightened awareness and consciousness. Everything mattered to Ignatius, and therefore, gradually, he began to discover the footprints and fingerprints of God in every aspect of his life. He even said in his autobiography that God had taught him like a teacher taught a student. Certainly, Ignatius was an exceptionally attentive pupil. Every moment became an awakening to God alive and present in his life and an awareness of his responses to this presence and more important—a moment of action. The combination of awakening, awareness, and action describes the meaning and dynamics of the contemplative experience.

Likewise, when I turn to the profile of the woman of the *Exercises* as described in this book, I notice a similar trajectory from awakening to action through awareness. She yearns for a liberating awakening. When she embarks on the adventure of the *Exercises*, she opens herself to grace and to God to gain a clearer awareness of the reality of God's presence in her life and to embrace the transformative actions for which that presence empowers her.

She is yearning for the freedom of God's dream and desire for her. She is seeking the will of God for her life but only so that she can respond accordingly in love and freedom and surrender to God's presence as a way of living and acting out God's will in her every experience as the *imago Dei*. The combination is as simple as it is empowering—awakening, awareness, and action. In this combination is the meaning of the contemplative experience in Ignatian spirituality.

Yet another way of looking at what it means to be contemplative is to see the woman of the *Exercises* as a seeker, a pilgrim, a traveler on the way. This notion or imagery of movement is a recurring theme in this book. To be contemplative is not a call to spiritual sedentarism or complacency, nor is it mindless activism. The woman of the *Exercises* desires so much more than what is offered or permitted her by religion or society or her faith community. She is awake to the belief that God has a fuller, deeper, and richer purpose for her.

Thanks to the gift of her imagination, she is aware that another world is possible for her. For this reason, her questions are probing, her desires are deep, and her horizons are wide.

Thus, the status quo does not satisfy her; she yearns for more—more of herself and more of her God. From the depths of her being wells up challenging inquiries: Who am I as a woman in my family, and with my friends, my colleagues, my career, my community, my job, my society, my faith, my country? Why am I here? What is life for me now? What is God revealing to me through the present circumstances of my life? What and who am I in relation to others, to nature, and to my God?

There are two things to note here. First, we can perceive echoes of what I presented in the preceding chapter about the strong link between awakening to the power to tell our own stories and the meaning of Principle and Foundation, how the former engenders the latter. Second, her questing and questioning lead her into a deeper awareness of who she is and who God is for her. This reminds me of a quote from Etty Hillesum's book *An Interrupted Life*, where she wrote from her prison cell:

> Perhaps my purpose in life is to come to grips with myself, properly to grips with myself, with everything that bothers and tortures me and clamors for inner solution and formulation for these problems are not just mine alone. And if at the end of a long life I am able to give some form to the chaos inside me, I may well have fulfilled my own small purpose...then I might perhaps find peace and clarity. But that would be no great feat. It is right here, in this very place, in the here and now, that I must find them.[1]

Here again we can discern aspects of the trilogy of awakening, awareness, and action as constitutive dimensions of the inner chaos that propels the contemplative quest of the woman of the *Exercises*.

As noted in chapter 3 regarding embodiment and friendship, in her journey of discovery, the woman of the *Exercises* gradually but ultimately discerns that the God of her desires is a lover and a friend. This God is not a man, a monarch, a judge, a ruler, or a prefabricated image superimposed on her being. The origin, truth, and foundation of her contemplative existence is simply that God wants to befriend her.

This reminds me of a scene from Antoine de Saint-Exupéry's fascinating book *The Little Prince*, in which a fox tells the prince that the way to become friends is to gaze upon each other in silence. For me, that is what being contemplative or practicing contemplation is about: returning God's loving gaze and becoming friends with the God of my life at all times and in all things with unencumbered freedom and boundless generosity and without bothering to find the right words or even saying a word, and much less even trying to give shape or form to this God.

Like the story of Jesus and the woman with the alabaster jar, contemplation is a journey of the heart: hearts speak to hearts in silence. Where the woman of the *Exercises* is, where she is from, or what she has done does not matter. God befriends her as she is and opens new pathways of love for her. Being a contemplative is responding to the invitation to meet the Divine and to reflect on her experiences under the loving gaze of God.

Seen in this light, life can hardly ever be boring or routine for the pilgrim striving to be a contemplative in action. Through the gaze of love fixed on the Divine, who returns this favor immeasurably, the woman of the *Exercises* will always discover new paths and new gifts. Her desires will be fuller and her longing truer to who she really is. Her dreams will exemplify more authentically God's dreams for her. In every situation, she will know that the Divine surrounds her with love. Like the prophet Zephaniah, she will know that, in all things and at all times, God will dance and rejoice over her and renew her with tenderness and love (see Zeph 3:17).

CONTEMPLATION TO ATTAIN LOVE/ SEEING GOD IN ALL THINGS

Keeping in mind what we have already noted about the trinity of awakening, awareness, and action, in this section, I illustrate the experience of being a contemplative in action and seeing God in all things using the form of prayer in the final exercise of the Fourth Week of the *Spiritual Exercises*. Ignatius christened this exercise "*Contemplatio ad amorem*," "Contemplation to attain love" (*Spiritual Exercises*, 230–37), albeit different writers have adopted their own translation. I believe that this four-part exercise gives us the most vivid picture of what it means to be contemplatives in action—to see God in all things and all things in God through awakening, awareness, and action. In its basic structure, it moves from seeing God as creator to seeing God as laboring to bring creation to birth and dwelling in creation and all creation being filled with the infinite graces, gifts, and goodness of God. At face value, it is easy to see this as a linear process or as an automatic process of emanation, but the exercise is much deeper and more engaging than that. Rather than giving a dry and detailed description, I invite readers to experience this exercise in a way that captures the triple movement of awakening, awareness, and action.

I invite you to relax and find a conducive place. Settle into a comfortable position. Pay attention to your breathing...in... and out. Become attuned to your surroundings and environment with all your senses....

Imagine yourself about to begin climbing a flight of stairs. As you approach the staircase, consider these words in your imagination:

> Divine love is with me here and now. Love is real and present in my life. Love fills my being....

Divine love is sharing love with me; love is connecting me with the Divine. Love is sharing everything with me; I am a beloved of God.

In your imagination, place your feet on the first step and begin to imagine your giftedness. How richly blessed you are. The many gifts you have received that have made you the person you are today. Just imagine the boundless, bottomless, and incomprehensible love that loved you into life. Imagine how much divine love has given you and continues to give you. Everything is yours for the love of God....

Move up higher, to the next step. Take a deep breath in... and out. Imagine the world around you. You are not alone. There is a vast tableau of creation that enfolds you, of which you are a part. That is not all. You and creation are lovingly fashioned by divine love. Divine love fills you with life and love; divine love holds, nurtures, and sustains you in life....

Take another step up the stairs. Imagine divine love surrounding you with everything you need in life and existence. Giving you breath, animating everything around you, quickening creatures into life so you can be nourished and sustained by them. Imagine divine love as a divine worker who does everything for you and delights that you are alive and here now....

Take another deep breath in...and out. Take one more step higher. Look around you and see the vast and immense expanse of your giftedness. Why are you so gifted? Why are you so beautiful? Why are you so unique? Imagine where all this is coming from. The inexhaustible source of divine love. Imagine divine love constantly, endlessly, lavishly pouring gifts upon gifts, love upon love, compassion upon compassion, tenderness upon tenderness, mercy upon mercy—everything on you for you to enjoy. Stay in this moment. Don't be in a hurry to move on. Enjoy and relish divine love enfolding you in an infinite embrace....

Now gradually begin to consider: How do I respond to this boundless, inexhaustible, and unfathomable love? What can I give in return?

Ignatius suggests a short prayer ("the Suscipe") of gratitude and generous offering:

Take, Lord, and receive all my liberty,
my memory, my understanding,
and my entire will,
All I have and call my own.

You have given all to me.
To you, Lord, I return it.

Everything is yours; do with it what you will.
Give me only your love and your grace,
that is enough for me.

Feel free to compose and use your own words to respond to this odyssey of endless love. Allow your heart filled with gratitude to speak directly to divine love....

This exercise is a love story, a story of how God's love becomes real in the life of God's creation. For the woman of the *Exercises*, it can be life changing to begin to see her life take shape as an oasis of infinite love. It means that her unique story, calling, and existence are important parts of God's plan in creation and that God is always gifting her. That she is not an accident of creation. That her life reflects God's infinite wisdom, goodness, and beauty. That she is awake to her giftedness and successes, and her challenges and accomplishments.

God's presence is neither dormant nor indifferent. God is active in every moment and in all the dimensions of her life. She is not defined and confined by the choices of her past. No. She is free, aware of, and open to the future of God's purposes for her. She sees God in all things. God is now personal to her in her experience of Jesus, the Divine. She finds creation suffused with the presence of this God. The creator is personal, and this awareness fills her with gratitude. It becomes her point of departure for her spirituality and her way of being and seeing.

She sees creation in a new way, not just as a beautiful, vast, lovely world but a world that "is charged with the grandeur of God," as the Jesuit poet, Gerard Manley Hopkins, discovered. Her being, uniqueness, existence, and creation become personal gifts inviting her to gratitude. She is a woman of the Spirit. She is becoming more attuned to her inner voice. She is able to discern the things of the Spirit in her life. She is growing into the knowledge that God is in love with her just as she is. She is growing into total dependence on God. Her world is richer and more sensible because she has come to know that God gazes on her with love and that she can respond with love.

There is a more profound truth here. It means that finally the woman of the *Exercises* now has a home—or as I always say, she has come home to herself. She is at home in God's heart, which is big enough to accommodate her joys and hopes, her pains and anxieties, her dreams and desires. She can now see God in every part of her life and see every part of her life in God. Contemplation to attain love is not a perfunctory task; attaining love is *coming home to God*. In the intimacy of this home, she can open herself fully to God without fear or hesitation; her spirit can grow and soar; and she can be content just to rest in God's love, knowing that God will neither exact payment nor impose conditions. God accepts and affirms her as she is.

As noted above, although Ignatius suggested a prayer formula called the Suscipe for responding to this experience, the woman of the *Exercises* is free to respond in any way the Spirit prompts her. She can respond by writing, painting, singing, dancing, cooking, baking, designing....Each one of these simple actions can become a celebration of her life, of who God is for her, and of her surrendering her deepest self in gratitude to divine love awake, aware, and alive.

Whenever I am privileged to accompany the woman of the *Exercises* who finds herself in this God-place of awakening, awareness, and action, I see the experience of spiritual companionship in a new light. Spiritual companionship is a shared journey. The two people are on a journey; both are pilgrims.

To the extent that the spiritual companion is awake to and aware of her own pilgrimage, she will be able to pay attention to, reverence, and honor the journey of the woman of the *Exercises*. Although Ignatius cautions the spiritual companion not to get in the way of the woman of the *Exercises* or interpose herself between her and her God, that should not stop the spiritual companion from placing herself on her path, alongside her, to affirm and to honor her quest as she comes home to herself. As mentioned in the preceding chapter, where God wants her to be is more important than where her spiritual companion wants her to be. With an open heart and an open mind, a spiritual companion will celebrate her every success and rejoice in her every step that brings her closer to who she is created to be in God.

THE GIFT OF DISCERNMENT

The exercise presented in the preceding section can be exhilarating, dizzying, and overwhelming. Its effect can be long-lasting. In the midst or in the aftermath of it, the woman of the *Exercises* can begin to see herself in a new light and even begin to make big and ambitious plans. This is normal. While Ignatius affirmed such generous and audacious outcomes, he was wise enough to counsel the retreatant to resist the temptation to be carried away by the warmth or afterglow of these moments of intense contemplative prayer. He suggested discerning the spirits that are setting us alight and urging us forward. Don't get carried away; test the spirit. This is wise and useful counsel.

Ignatius has several sections in the *Exercises* where he proposes and explains various rules for discerning and testing the spirits; they are suitable for different stages or dispositions of the retreatant. I believe that Ignatius's rules for discernment are a gift to women who embark on the adventure of the *Exercises*. Part of the triad of awakening, awareness, and action is becoming adept at spotting the patterns and trajectories of the movements in our interior states, attitudes, and dispositions to better align ourselves with the action of the God of our lives.

Discernment is an indispensable part of the adventure of the *Exercises*. As noted repeatedly, the woman who embarks on this journey comes as a person of many desires and longings. She comes with her being, the person she is. She does not come as one who considers herself as complete or finished. Rather, she comes as one who is in the process of knowing, discovering, and growing. She is on her way, and she yearns for new personal vistas and guidance into new insights. She is God's ongoing creation. She is the clay in the hands of the potter allowing herself to be shaped and reshaped—formed and reformed and transformed.

What does discernment entail for the woman of the *Exercises*, and why is it important? The process of discernment or choice-making depends significantly on the woman's knowledge of herself. Her choice-making will come only from her self-knowledge and identity. The key word here is the possessive *her*. As mentioned in chapter 2, this knowledge is experiential and holistic, not intellectual or compartmentalized. For her, discernment spans the gamut of her personality, her experiences, her desires, and her longings.

When it comes to discernment, the pivotal questions that emerge for her are: What is God doing in this situation with me? Where does God desire to lead me through this experience? Yet, as noted in previous chapters, many women have unfortunately been alienated from their true feelings and desires by a conspiracy of cultural, religious, and societal factors. Consequently, they feel homeless and unable to be comfortable with their true feelings. What accounts for this? There are several reasons as we can surmise from our discussion. Let me recap a few.

The woman who embarks on the journey of the *Spiritual Exercises* might come from a culture that has muted her person and voice. She might be acting only on the impulse of what her culture, religion, and society expect of her. Sadly, this might be interpreted by her and the culture, religion, and society in which she lives as the understanding of what it means to be a "good" woman.

An apt example of this contrived definition is the profile of a virtuous wife in Proverbs 31:10–31. Whether married or religious, a woman who dares to challenge such cultural, religious, and societal norms and expectations risks losing her sense of self and becoming an outcast. Ignatian discernment offers an effective means of untangling the stranglehold of these norms on her life; it allows her to see what spirits flourish her and what spirits diminish her so she can embrace the former and reject the latter.

The woman of the *Exercises* can feel joy and experience pain, but like the cricket in the proverb cited in chapter 4, she may choose to contain or repress these feelings because she has been taught not to focus on herself. Such distortion of her emotional capacity translates into spiritual homelessness. She loses her personal identity and deep sense of the presence of her loving God, who is always there beckoning her to return home. When she engages in Ignatian discernment, she can trace and follow the path that will bring her home to herself and to the God of her life.

Recall that the woman of the *Exercises* is not just a spiritual being; she is also an incarnate being. She has a physical presence. She is the *imago Dei*. Yet cultural, religious, and societal norms can impair her ability to experience the fullness of her mystical and Christic identity. She may be deprived of weeping those tears that Ignatius describes as the tears of consolation (*Spiritual Exercises*, 322). If she is unable to cry those tears, like the woman with the alabaster jar, she will be unable to love herself. She is obstructed in her relationship with God and in her ability to enjoy God's immeasurable love. She can be at home only through her desires and intuitions, her yearnings and feelings. Unable to notice and understand these deeper realities, she will never be able to discern where God is with her. The Spirit is constrained from within. No wonder Ignatius said, "Pray for the desire to desire." Without a deep sense of knowing, the woman will never be able to discern what her true calling is from God.

The foregoing shows some of the many ways that cultural, religious, and societal norms have structured the life of the woman of the *Exercises*. Often, her tears are tears of guilt, not of consolation for the undeserved love of God. The process of discernment with the help of a spiritual companion allows her to grow and to experience what gives her life or denies her life. She can gradually discern correctly what is life affirming and see the injustices that are being heaped on her by others. The difference between both instances is the difference between consolation and desolation. Not only does she discern the difference, she is also empowered to embrace the former and reject the latter.

It helps for the woman of the *Exercises* to engage in the path of discernment not from the limited ways that Ignatius proposes as good angels and spirits versus bad angels and spirits. She is free to examine the totality of her life experience to see where darkness obscures light, death tramples life, and pain deprives her of joy. With practice and repetition, she will grow in her awareness of those movements in her and recognize the causes and the consequent experiences flowing from those causes. Increasingly, she will recognize with greater clarity the sources of her joy and the subject of her love, hope, and faith—

the very manifestations of consolation. She will not deny the existence of the sources of her pain and anxiety; she will learn not to be enslaved or ruled by them. She will know that her life is unfolding at a deeper level, just as Ignatius's did while on his sickbed, when God is peeling back the fleeting and false emotions and desires to reveal deeper and lasting pointers to God's presence and action in her life.

Enlivened and emboldened by the good spirits, she can begin to celebrate the signs of her beauty as the *imago Dei*, to identify the moments of her giftedness, and to resist the burden of falsehoods created around her. She can resolve to listen to only life-giving spirits even in times of pain or anxiety and remain awake to and be aware of the will of God for her and what actions and choices are commensurate with this will.

Thanks to the gift of discernment, she becomes the captain of her soul and owner of her dreams, thus able to grow into a space and place where she will embrace the outcomes that these insights provide for her and others' lives. Like St. Irenaeus, she will know that the glory of God is the human person and all creation fully alive.

The gift of discernment for the woman of the *Exercises* consists of an invitation to an awakening to and awareness of the desires and movements in her and the actions and choices they engender. It is an awakening to and an awareness of the direction of instances, events, and moments of her life that either draw her into the depths and tenderness of God's love or alienate her from it. Again, as noted, she can celebrate the former and discard the latter.

Ignatian discernment is a *process* of paying attention to the spirits working in the life of the woman of the *Exercises*. It is a learning experience that grows with the Ignatian methodology of practiced repetition. This sense of discernment needs to be developed especially in the beginning of her journey to becoming alert, to choosing a more focused life whenever the challenges of society, culture, family, and career take life away from her. She must plan to rise to her own deepest desires as the way of responding to that situation. She must learn to say no to situations that do not give her life. And she must learn to trust that in her actions and her waiting, God will lead her to life. She will not always have the outcomes she desires and longs for. The bad spirits are clever and cunning, says Ignatius. They can turn up as angels of light.

Some women find themselves tricked into situations in which they are vulnerable. I recall a story of a woman who was struggling in her marriage because of poverty. She was approached by a rich man who was willing to give her the money she needed to support her family ostensibly because he was impressed and moved by her good works as an outstanding teacher of his child. When he invited her to have lunch with him, he suggested that she sleep with him. She found herself struggling with this offer. After all, he had been so kind to her in response to her work with his child, but she was very disturbed about the idea of compromising her moral integrity to bring in money for her family. The initial consolation of joy and happiness she had experienced through the idea of making money to feed her family gradually disappeared. The angel of darkness had appeared under the guise of light, as one who wanted to help her. But gradually, she discerned the true colors of this angel and realized that this man was trying to buy her body and destroy her soul.

Likewise, the woman of the *Exercises* will grow in her awareness of the wiles and guiles of the evil spirit clothed in light. Like Ignatius, through discernment, she will grow in her capacity to reflect on the subtleties of her spirit and ask probing questions about the kind of spirits present in her spiritual experience. Even amid her confusion and anxiety, she must remain patient and reach deep into stored-up graces of previous moments of consolation to wait out the storm, clear the fog, and expose the deceits of the bad spirits. This was how Ignatius was able to understand God's workings in his life.

It is not out of place for the woman of the *Exercises* to feel the pangs of desolation that many reasons can explain. However, no matter the origin, reason, or cause, the important thing to keep in mind is that God is never far away; divinity may hide itself, but it has not disappeared. Patience is a key ingredient in discernment. The consolation of God is not the same as the God of consolation. The pursuit of the former can impede the encounter with the latter.

In the perspective of Ignatian spirituality, desolation can strengthen spirituality and nurture humility. Consolation and desolation are God's initiatives according to Ignatius. However, the woman of the *Exercises* is invited to know that she is the temple of God. She is the house of the Spirit of God where consolation and desolation are both experienced. She is called to be attentive to God's mysterious workings as expressed through her daily life. A useful Ignatian maxim to keep in mind is that only God can give consolation without a preceding cause (*Spiritual Exercises*, 330).

ODDS AGAINST HER

A blatant manifestation of gender prejudice and stereotyping appears in the text of Ignatius's *Spiritual Exercises*. In one of his rules for discernment, Ignatius compares the antics of the evil spirit to the behavior of a woman. "He conducts himself like a woman," says Ignatius, "weak when faced by firmness but strong in the face of acquiescence" (*Spiritual Exercises*, 325). In another instance, he alludes to women as fickle and easily misled by the evil one acting secretively as "a false lover" (*Spiritual Exercises*, 326).

As noted in chapter 1, Ignatius was a man of his times steeped in an egregious mire of patriarchy, sexism, and misogyny.

I could pick a quarrel with his prejudicial and damaging association of women with evil spirits. While that could be an intellectually satisfying exercise, I choose, as I have done throughout this book, to write and talk about the *Spiritual Exercises* on my own terms and in ways that are spiritually fulfilling and empowering for women who desire to find and encounter the God of their lives rather than be misled by the idols of their culture, religion, and society propped up by such fallacious and dangerous misrepresentations. I believe that women can reclaim the legacy of the *Spiritual Exercises* on their own terms, including naming where it fails to honor their integrity, dignity, and worth as the *imago Dei*.

Thus, through the gift and practice of discernment, the woman of the *Exercises* can grow in embracing the beauty, truth, and goodness of who she is as a beloved of God. She can become present to every movement in her heart and in the experiences that she has with others. By paying attention to her feelings, desires, dreams, and emotions, she can discover how these are the raw materials for discerning God's presence in her life and God's will for her.

Discernment for a woman of the *Exercises* does not happen in a vacuum. The milieu in which her life is unfolding can be quite inimical to her desires and longings and present multiple impediments or challenges to her growth and fulfillment. She may be living her life in response to the warped expectations of her culture, religion, and society, or be so committed to what she has absorbed from her surroundings that she can hardly perceive the differences in her own desires. She might have been raised in a faith tradition that does not give her the room to think or imagine for herself.

But thanks to the liberating dynamics of Ignatian spirituality she finds in the *Spiritual Exercises*, she is invited to listen to the power of her true self. She is challenged to trust her intuition and her desires and feelings. This is where God is calling her to God's desires for her. By cultivating this kind of discerning spirit, she can reflect more freely and deeply within, to sit with her inner movements and feelings, to uncover deep wells within that have been there but undiscovered. This experience banishes all fear or hesitation in accepting the truth that she is God's delight, and that God wants to be her story and wants to weave her unique story into the beautiful tapestry of God's creation. It is a liberating experience that empowers her to discern the difference between the angels of light and the demons of darkness even if or when the latter occasionally disguise themselves as the former.

The practice of discernment for the woman of the *Exercises* is fraught with many hurdles and obstacles. In a culture, religion, or society in which women's voices do not always matter, she will need time and patience to learn to trust her inner wisdom, knowledge, and intuition. One of the greatest gifts that a spiritual companion can offer her is the gentle invitation to trust what is going on in her and her desires and longings.

One woman saw signs that her husband was cheating on her and felt he could harm their marriage. She felt the abuse of a man who was no longer emotionally present to her, but she was afraid to confront him. For years, she stayed with a man who would neither engage with her nor acknowledge her existence. Although she was able to share with a trusted companion the pain and the desolation of this situation, she did not trust her own judgment; she contented herself with the church's teaching forbidding divorce. In addition, she believed that her culture would not accept a divorced woman.

Unhappy and depressed, she did not trust herself to make any decision because of her commitment to church and society. However, if she could make this brave decision to confront her husband, she might be able to see how she had condoned the bad spirits leading to desolation. She might be able to start over with a new life again.

As a woman in such a situation coming to the space of the *Spiritual Exercises,* she will need to be gently supported to trust her voice and to hear the Spirit in calling her to more of what she can be and was created to be. Her world will be much bigger and richer when she can trust her inner eye and her inner conviction about who she is called to be. It will be a precious gift if she can find her point of departure and source of courage in making decisions from within.

A GUIDED MEDITATION

I invite readers to engage in a simple exercise of discernment. Ignatius offers one of the simplest and most easily understood definitions of consolation and desolation. As he puts it in his third rule for the discernment of spirits:

> Under the word consolation I include every increase in hope, faith, and charity, and every interior joy which calls and attracts one toward heavenly things and to the salvation of one's soul, by bringing it tranquility and peace in its Creator and God.

Desolation, of course, means "everything which is the contrary of what was described in the Third Rule" (*Spiritual Exercises,* 316–17). It is that simple. How astute are you in distinguishing what causes you consolation from what causes you desolation?

Find a conducive location and assume a comfortable position. Take a few deep breaths. Pay attention to your senses and through them become aware of and attuned to your surroundings and environment....

Gradually begin to recall the moments of your day. Moment by moment, hour by hour, place by place, and person by person. Notice the events of each moment, each hour, and each place. See the people who were part of each moment....

Pay attention to your feelings in relation to these moments, events, places, and people. What emotions surface? Are there some moments, events, people, or places that make you swell with joy and delight? Are there some moments, events, people, or places that deflate your joy and make you sad? Continue to move from one situation to the other, and back and forth....

In each of these varying situations, pay attention to what the inner voice is telling you. Stay with where you feel your faith is increasing, your hope is expanding, and your love is deepening. Gradually begin to formulate and address a prayer from the depths of your heart. From the depths of your feelings and emotions, allow your heart to speak to your God about the people, places, and events that make your day.

Conclusion:
An Unfolding Story

A calabash in constant use will be stitched and mended.

—An African proverb

The *Spiritual Exercises of St. Ignatius of Loyola* was formally approved in 1548 by Pope Paul III. For nearly five hundred years and except for minor emendations Ignatius made to it, the manual of the *Exercises* has remained in use without any notable modification to its content and structure. With an enduring appeal, this spiritual classic has stood the test of time. Like an indispensable vessel in constant use, it has been stitched and mended through several translations, interpretations, and applications. Yet it has remained a resilient and fascinating receptacle of Ignatian spirituality as the latter has evolved, developed, and spread across the globe.

Throughout this book, I have shared my experiences of, perspectives on, encounters with, and appreciation for Ignatian spirituality in its quintessential representation in the *Spiritual Exercises*. Underlying my narrative is the personal and deep conviction that women and the *Spiritual Exercises of St. Ignatius* are not strangers. Women shaped Ignatius's spiritual trajectory and influenced the *Exercises* and everything we recognize as Ignatian spirituality. To some, this might sound like a monumental claim or exaggeration, but it is a deeply held conviction derived from my experiences and those of many women whose spiritual journey I have been privileged to be associated with in my ministry as a spiritual companion.

Ignatian spirituality offers women a valuable instrument for overcoming the troubles they sometimes must contend with in their quest for a meaningful and fulfilling encounter with the God of their lives. This instrument can be worn, stitched, and mended, but it remains a precious vessel of gifts and graces. I believe that, were Ignatius to see what a splendid thing women have made and continue to make of Ignatian spirituality and the *Spiritual Exercises*, he would concede that woman trouble is good trouble!

To recap some essential points, the *Spiritual Exercises* offer many women who long to come home to themselves a path of a deep, transforming, and life-affirming encounter with the Divine. This path is not as daunting or esoteric as it might first appear. Properly understood, the journey of the *Exercises* honors the uniqueness, desires, and longings of the woman of the *Exercises*—who she is and how God desires to lead her to a place of an intimate encounter. In this sense, Ignatian spirituality is infinitely adaptable. This is good news for the woman of the *Exercises*, precisely because any means or methods of praying—scripture texts, images, poetry, skills, talents, or nature—can be adopted, tried, adapted, modified, or changed to find the most suitable means of gently leading her to a deeper affirmation and celebration of her beauty, worth, goodness, and giftedness.

Engaging with Ignatian spirituality calls for creativity and flexibility so that the woman of the *Exercises* can profit by way of an abundance of graces, blessings, and consolations, all of which can be profoundly renewing and liberating for her in her adventure of the *Exercises*. Essentially, for the woman of the *Exercises*, nothing short of the discovery and celebration of herself as created in the image and likeness of God will do as an outcome of this journey. There is a reason that the woman of the *Exercises* embarks on this exhilarating journey.

As I have mentioned, she desires to discover who she is and who God wants her to become. As Ignatius mentions in the explanatory notes for the *Spiritual Exercises*, the *Exercises* offers "every way" of preparing and baring her soul to the transformative touch of God even if it means walking, wandering, jumping, or running (*Spiritual Exercises*, 1).

In the genius of Ignatius, even the guidelines, instructions, and directives for making the *Spiritual Exercises* are not carved in stone. That is why he always hedges them with the Latin expression *tantum quantum*, that is, use them insofar as they are helpful, insofar as they bear good fruits. This spirit of flexibility and adaptability may be a manifestation of the legacy of the influence of the women in Ignatius's life. Through this quality, the woman of the *Exercises* can begin to discover God not in all things in general but in the depths of her soul, in the song of her heart, in the story of her dreams, and in the dance of life all with the God who has called her into life by name.

For spiritual companions who have the privilege and honor of accompanying the woman of the *Exercises* on her journey, the focus should rest solidly on her quest to acquire a clearer and more empowering vision of who God is for her and of who she is called to be for her God. Honoring this vision is a sacred trust. It is important to be discerning in choosing and proposing images and scripture texts or prayer patterns with due consideration for her personality, her story, and her desires.

Because the *Spiritual Exercises* is based on scripture and adapts it for the purposes of the user, it helps to be alert to how biblical texts function in individual circumstances as well as in the cultural, religious, and social contexts of women in general.

In proposing scripture texts to the woman of the *Exercises*, we should be mindful of latent patterns of gender biases, including sexism, in the texts but also the potential of scripture to uplift women's voices, affirm their dignity, and transform them into bearers of the image and likeness of God when approached critically and creatively. It is never permissible to use scripture to diminish or distort women's images or perceptions of themselves.

Storytelling creates a safe and inviting space for the woman of the *Exercises* to recover her voice, to construct her narrative, and to tell her story in her own voice. For her story to be authentic, empowering, and liberating, she ought to be enabled to deploy the gift of her imagination with creativity, confidence, and audacity. In doing so, she will not be afraid to unearth and tell her hidden and untold stories.

To recall the wise words of the late African American writer Maya Angelou, "A bird does not sing because it has an answer, it sings because it has a song." Likewise, the woman of the *Exercises* does not pray because she knows the answer; she prays because she has a story. The ability to tell her story confers on her the power to confront the distorted stories that others, including agents of culture, religion, and society, have constructed and spoken about her. Crucially, in her Ignatian adventure, her story can take many forms as she uses all her gifts, talents, and blessings to compose, weave, design, sing, dance, or bake her story. In such a space, whoever is privileged to accompany her or witness her moments of intimate encounter with the Divine will do well to maintain a spirit of reverence, patience, and a listening heart to welcome, affirm, and honor her story.

Thus, in the pilgrimage of discovery of the woman of the *Exercises*, no one may assume or usurp her voice. As a spiritual companion, I understand my role as one of offering the requisite hospitality for her to feel comfortable enough to tell her story with her own voice and from her own heart. Again, this requires the gift of deep listening and patience in accompanying her to discern her gifts and her paths.

One very interesting thing I have discovered in my ministry of spiritual companionship is that, for Ignatius, this spiritual journey is mutually beneficial. In fact, from experience, the woman of the *Exercises* is a gift to me as well. She is fully and completely the *imago Dei* from whom I can also learn. We both share this privileged common identity and status. Ignatius insists that God gifts and graces the soul with an abundance of consolation. The woman of the *Exercises* will find this consolation and be comforted if through the gift of my listening she has been heard, because she is a living person; she is a courageous adventurer. She is fully alive with a soul that desires and yearns passionately for her God. In this process of self-discovery, she becomes a gift for me as well.

To reiterate, part of the beauty of the *Spiritual Exercises* is that Ignatius composed it to be adaptable and adapted to conditions of persons, times, and places. One of Ignatius's basic rules is to be ready to adapt it to the needs of the person in accordance with her or his greater or lesser degree of progress. This entails a capacity on the part of the spiritual companion to listen deeply and to witness patiently to the situation in life of the woman and to quieten our inner voices so that we can attend to her unique identity and substance. This kind of attitude entails resisting any desire to force her into a prefabricated mold. A useful maxim to note is that where God wants to lead her is more important than where anybody else, including spiritual companions, wants her to go.

The greatest gift the woman of the *Exercises* brings to prayer is the uniqueness, giftedness, mystery, and sacredness of her body. She was created in the *imago Dei* to praise, reverence, and serve God, and none of this makes sense without immersing herself in the encounter with the Divine with all her feelings, imagination, intellect, and emotions. The *Spiritual Exercises* is an embodied instrument of prayer; we see this in so many aspects of the *Exercises*, including the composition of place, the application of the senses, the posture of prayer, and the colloquy. Along with the imagination, the gift of embodiment opens a path to spiritual friendship that is unique because the feelings and emotions of the woman of the *Exercises* are essential gifts for preparing and disposing her soul to enter an intimate relationship with the Divine.

Ignatian spirituality takes us on a journey of love into a deeper discovery of God who dwells in every step, every moment, and every experience of our lives. When one is privileged to accompany others on this journey as a spiritual companion, one's goal is always to be present to the pilgrimage of the woman of the *Exercises* with sensitivity, patience, attention, devotion, and reverence. Finding God in all things and seeing all things in God is a lifelong contemplative experience. It is an unfolding story of how God dwells in us, and we dwell in God. This awareness gives the woman of the *Exercises* the confidence, joy, courage, and hope to continue to dream and to desire to find God in all aspects of her life.

To be contemplative in action is to come home to ourselves and to our God. God's heart is our true home; God's heart is an inexhaustible font of love. As a popular song goes, God's love is so high we can never get over it, so deep we can never get under it, so wide we can never get around it. What a wonderful love! Discovering this love is the greatest source of joy and gratitude for those who embark on the adventure of the *Spiritual Exercises*.

Ignatian spirituality entails a mystical inclusiveness. Everything matters—our stories and desires, our bodies and ourselves—everything is space for prayer, a place for God to encounter us. Being contemplative is the equivalent of being deeply awakened, fully aware, and passionately active under

God's gaze and grace. Yet being in touch with the Divine does not immobilize or paralyze us. Quite the opposite. The encounter energizes, inspires, enables, and emboldens us to embody and reflect the presence and energy of the Divine in our world, in our choices and decisions, actions and responses, dreams and stories. This is the triple trajectory of awakening, awareness, and action. It is never one without the others. Ignatian spirituality offers a means for discovering this path and striking out on it with confidence, joy, courage, and hope.

A GUIDED MEDITATION

I invite readers to invoke and celebrate with gratitude the mothers of Ignatian spirituality and of the *Spiritual Exercises* whose journey we have shared in this book as pilgrims.

As usual, find a conducive space and assume a comfortable position. Take a few deep breaths and become attuned to your surroundings or environment with all your senses....

Imagine yourself standing in front of and surrounded by all the women in the life of St. Ignatius of Loyola. They form a formidable cloud of witnesses....

Remember the entire household of Loyola and especially the domestic workers, mostly women, who took care of Iñigo and in various ways influenced Ignatius and the formation of the *Spiritual Exercises*....

Remember all the women described in generic terms in the accounts of the life of Ignatius, women who were influential beyond words in his life, women of every class, status, and estate....

Remember women who were generous benefactresses of Ignatius and who supported him in his spiritual pilgrimage and assisted him with his material needs; several who gave him alms and many who visited him in jail or in hospital, and in return benefitted from his spiritual accompaniment, wise counsel, and fervent prayers....

Remember several women who asked to be admitted into the Society of Jesus by a reluctant Ignatius—some who were admitted and others who were not—but all who left their imprint on the life of Ignatius and Ignatian spirituality....

Surrounded by all these women of passion, depth, and substance, repeat this prayer slowly, gratefully, until you are satisfied:

I remember you, mothers of Ignatius and mothers of
  the *Spiritual Exercises*.
I thank you, mothers of Ignatius and mothers of the
  Spiritual Exercises.
I remember you. Amen!

Notes

INTRODUCTION: WOMAN TROUBLE

1. St. Ignatius Loyola, *The Spiritual Exercises of Saint Ignatius*, trans. and com. George E. Ganss, SJ (St. Louis, MO: The Institute of Jesuit Sources, 1992). Unless otherwise indicated, references to the *Exercises* are taken from this edition.

2. Hugo Rahner, ed., *St. Ignatius Loyola: Letters to Women* (New York: Herder & Herder/Crossroad, 1960).

3. Margaret Silf, *Inner Compass: An Invitation to Ignatian Spirituality* (Chicago: Loyola Press, 2007); Joyce Rupp, *Open the Door: A Journey to the True Self* (Notre Dame, IN: Sorin Books, 2008); Elizabeth Johnson, *She Who Is: The Mystery of God in Feminist Theological Discourse* (New York: Crossroad, 2002).

4. Katherine Dyckman, Mary Garvin, and Elizabeth Liebert, *The Spiritual Exercises Reclaimed: Uncovering Liberating Possibilities for Women* (Mahwah, NJ: Paulist Press, 2001).

5. See https://www.ignatianspirituality.com/the-women -in-st-ignatiuss-life/; see also https://youtu.be/lZ_exqpA74U/.

6. William A. Barry, SJ, and Robert G. Doherty, SJ, *Contemplatives in Action: The Jesuit Way* (Mahwah, NJ: Paulist Press, 2002); Kevin O'Brien, *The Ignatian Adventure: Experiencing the Spiritual Exercises of St. Ignatius in Daily Life* (Chicago: Loyola

Press, 2011); Howard Gray, "A Jesuit Retreat with Howard Gray" (Audio CD).

1. IN THE BEGINNING WERE WOMEN

1. Rogelio Garcia-Mateo, SJ, "Ignatius of Loyola and Women," *Theology Digest* 45, no. 1 (1998): 27–32.
2. Rahner, ed., *Letters to Women*, 173–74.
3. Adapted from Rahner, *Letters to Women*, 287.

3. WOMEN'S BODIES AND THE GOD OF OUR BODIES

1. "Message to the People of God of the Second Special Assembly for Africa of the Synod of Bishops," October 23, 2009, no. 25, https://www.vatican.va/roman_curia/synod/documents/rc_synod_doc_20091023_message-synod_en.html.
2. Tina Beattie, "A Mother Is Born: A Reflection in Four Parts," paper delivered to Yale Center for Faith & Culture consultation on "Birth and Human Flourishing," October 2015, see https://www.youtube.com/watch?v=3KjaW4ZF59I.
3. Junno Arocho Esteves, "Pope Francis Raises Memorial of St. Mary Magdalene to a Feast Day," Catholic News Service, June 10, 2016, https://www.americamagazine.org/faith/2016/06/10/pope-francis-raises-memorial-st-mary-magdalene-feast-day.
4. Robert Cardinal Sarah, "Decree," Prot. N. 257/16, 2016, https://www.vatican.va/roman_curia/congregations/ccdds/documents/sanctae-m-magdalenae-decretum_en.pdf.
5. "Preface of the Apostle of the Apostles," excerpt from the English translation of *The Roman Missal* © 2010 ICEL. All rights reserved, https://www.usccb.org/prayer-and-worship/

liturgical-year-and-calendar/saint-mary-magdalene (accessed March 8, 2022).

6. Pope Francis, "Prayer for the Extraordinary Jubilee of Mercy," December 8, 2015, https://www.vatican.va/content/francesco/en/prayers/documents/papa-francesco_preghiere_20151208_giubileo-straordinario-misericordia.html.

7. Stephen Rooke, dir., "Flesh and Blood," ep. 1, *Decoding Christianity* (Dublin, Ireland: Tile Films, 2008).

8. Elizabeth Johnson, *Women, Earth, and Creator Spirit*, rev. ed. (Mahwah, NJ: Paulist Press, 2022).

4. THE GIFT AND THE GOD OF IMAGINATION

1. Gustavo Gutierrez, *The God of Life* (Maryknoll, NY: Orbis Books, 1991), 90.

2. Kofi Appiah-Kubi, "Oh Mother Earth," *Zygon* 19, no. 1 (1984): 61–63, at 61.

5. THE GOD-PLACE OF STORYTELLING

1. Chimamanda Ngozi Adichie, "The Danger of a Single Story," TED, 2009, accessed May 21, 2021, https://www.ted.com/talks/chimamanda_ngozi_adichie_the_danger_of_a_single_story.

2. Elder Mullan, SJ, "The First Principle and Foundation from the Spiritual Exercises [23] of Ignatius of Loyola—A Literal Translation," ed. Rick Rossi, March 2015, https://www.bc.edu/content/dam/files/offices/ministry/pdf.

3. John Paul II, "General Audience," January 30, 2002, no. 6, https://www.vatican.va/content/john-paul-ii/en/audiences/2002/documents/hf_jp-ii_aud_20020130.html.

6. CONTEMPLATIVE AWAKENING, AWARENESS, AND ACTION

1. Etty Hillesum, *An Interrupted Life: The Diaries, 1941–1943 and Letters from Westerbork* (New York: Henry Holt and Company, 1996), 36.